Traditional Needlework
in Miniature

Classic Designs with 54 Patterns

By Annelle Ferguson

16th-Century English to
19th-Century American Embroidery

Cover photo: Wing chair in 1-inch-to-the-foot scale designed and constructed by Charles Krug. Needlework designed by Annelle Ferguson. Tea table and Chippendale side chair by Gerald Crawford, tea service by Peter Acquisto, candlestick by Emily Good, floorcloth by Ann Miller. *Photographer: Mary Kaliski*

Photo on this page: Interpretative adaptation of a 1772 Boston sampler worked by Annelle Ferguson on #60 silk gauze using silk sewing thread. Motifs of deer being chased by dogs are also found on several "Fishing Lady" series canvas worked pieces. From the collection of Sarah Salisbury. *Photo courtesy of Annelle Ferguson*

Photo on back cover: 1-inch-scale living room setting from the Nelson Kline collection. Game table, chairs and firescreen crafted by Charles Krug. Needlework chair seats and firescreen panel designed and stitched by Annelle Ferguson on #60 silk gauze using silk sewing thread.
Each pattern has a different rural setting: Shepherdess and Piper, Lady and Gentleman, Maiden and Peasant, Milkmaid and Huntsman. Designs are interpretative adaptations of four original chair seats, two in Boston's Museum of Fine Arts and two in Delaware's Winterthur Museum, Garden & Library. Such rural designs, surrounded by a floral border, were popular in 18th-century America. *Photo by Mary and Tom Kaliski*

Book Team
Editor: Barbara J. Aardema
Book Design: Anne Huizenga
Photography: Tom Smith, unless otherwise credited

First Edition 2003
Copyright ©2003 by Scott Publications
ISBN: 1-893625-06-0
Library of Congress Control Number: 2003100162

Published by
©2003
SCOTT PUBLICATIONS
801 W. Norton Avenue, Suite 200
Muskegon, MI 49441

PRINTED IN CHINA

Photo by Oak Ridge Portraits

Annelle Ferguson is a self-taught needleworker who began stitching by making needle-point rugs for her daughter's dollhouse. With her 1-inch-scale needleworks, she has earned the rank of Fellow in the International Guild of Miniature Artisans, an organization for which she is a past president. She has taught at Guild School and Guild Study Programs various times since 1989.

Annelle has been named to the Academy of Honor by the National Association of Miniature Enthusiasts and she is the United States representative to the Miniature Needlework Society. She has been in business since 1986 under the name Mini Stitches.

Acknowledgements

To the generous mind the heaviest debt is that of gratitude, when it is not in our power to repay it.—Benjamin Franklin (1706-1790)

Photo by Jason Getzan

Detail of clock case vignette designed by Frank Hanley and Jeffrey Guéno for Sarah Salisbury.

The writing of this book was made possible with help from many very talented people. I was able to rely on old friends who generously gave of their time to create specific projects, and along the way, I made new friends who willingly agreed to create requested designs. It has been a delight to work with so many needlework artisans who share a common bond—a love for miniature needlework. I am especially grateful to Anne Chauvin, Martha (Stubby) Crowe, Clarice Elder, Sharon Garmize, Shirlee Greenberg, Jessie Harrison, Lucy Iducovich, Judith Kaelin, Judith Ohanian, Esther Robertson, Bobbie Schoonmaker, Erma Scrimgeour, Susan Sirkis, Nancy Sturgeon, Pat Tulski, Duffy Wineman, and Cookie Ziemba for allowing me to recognize their talents and creativity. The 17th-century casket, designed by Bill Robertson and covered in needlework by his mother, Esther, was a requested project that both graciously accepted. Bill created a unique frame for the 17th-century mirror surround. It is a thrill to have the charming sampler from Barbara Cosgrove. Barbara is responsible for introducing me to antique needlework, which was certainly a turning point in my needlepoint designing. I am so pleased to show the work of Virginia Merrill. I have always considered Barbara, Virginia, and Clarice Elder as my mentors. As a self-taught needleworker, I was able to sharpen my skills using patterns produced by each of them.

Sarah Salisbury is responsible for introducing me to Daphne Turner. It is an honor to show Daphne's beautiful needlework. She and her husband, Ivan, are very dear to me. Daphne, in turn, introduced me to the works of Sue Bakker, Ann Crompton, and Rosemary Conway-Jones from the United Kingdom. Having each of them share their exquisite designs has truly given this project an international flavor. A sincere thank you to Lanto Synge of Malletts, Ltd. in London for allowing Sue Bakker to create a carpet based on one in their collection.

I am equally pleased to show the beautiful work of other talented needleworkers: Mitzi Van Horn, Lynda Bauer, Jean Strup, Rosemary Hansen and Sarah Anne Evans. I appreciate Emily Good, The Toy and Miniature Museum of Kansas City, and The Chipstone Foundation for loaning photographs from their collections. A very sincere thank you to Glee Kruger for allowing me to create a 1:12-scale sampler based on an original in her collection. Other collectors, such as Nelson Kline and Peter Kendall, allowed photographs to be taken of their room settings decorated with needlework.

The furniture makers were indispensable in providing the perfect piece for specific projects. Thank you to David Booth, Gerald Crawford, Wayne Crosby, Tom Goad, Roger Gutheil, Carol Hardy, Donna and Jim Johnson, Charles Krug, Linda LaRoche and Betty Valentine. My dear friend, Margaret Nine, framed all samplers and embroidered pictures for me. I appreciate Duffy Wineman and Debbie Sloan for allowing photographs of their full-size antique needlework.

Over a decade ago, I became consumed with researching antique needlework in order to apply the styles from different periods to my miniature needlework. I knew early on that I wanted to share with the miniature industry the knowledge acquired from my readings and my visits to museums and historical societies. Sarah Salisbury, one person whom I truly look up to and admire, was the first to encourage me onward. Sarah introduced me to Anne Day Smith and so began a lasting friendship. Anne, an experienced writer, was able to advise and guide me in the right direction for producing such a publication. I am deeply indebted to both for their support and inspiration. Anne also graciously helped with photographing various items and room settings. My special friendship with Mary Kaliski began while serving on the Board of Trustees for the International Guild of Miniature Artisans. I will forever be grateful to Mary and her husband, Tom, for providing the majority of the beautiful photographs in this publication. I appreciate the efforts of Jason Getzan, Kevin Hosley, Peter Charman, and Daemon for also providing exceptional photographs of special needleworked items.

I am greatly indebted to Ruth Keessen for her belief in the concept and idea of sharing with the miniature industry a brief history of needlework. A very special and sincere thank you to Barbara Aardema for her expertise in editing the material presented. It has been a pleasure working with her. I give my heartfelt appreciation and gratitude to all who helped me turn my dream into a reality. Finally, to Jim Ferguson, for his constant encouragement and support throughout this endeavor.

Contents

Band of cross-stitch near top of full-size Sarah Lowell antique sampler. Collection of Glee Kruger.

Band of cross-stitch near bottom of full-size Sarah Lowell antique sampler. Collection of Glee Kruger.

Photos by Mary and Tom Kaliski

Preface

We are shaped and fashioned by what we love.
—Johann Wolfgang von Goethe (1749-1832)

Photos by Mary and Tom Kaliski

The full-size sampler, stitched by 8-year-old Mary Ann Cole in 1848, is from the collection of Sylvia Rountree. The design may be from an English day school for orphaned children.

Annelle Ferguson worked a miniature version of the Mary Ann Cole sampler on #60 silk gauze.

The history of needlework spans thousands of years. Embroidered items were produced in virtually every civilized country in the world; however, the origin of needlework as a craft is lost in history. Primitive man used a splinter of bone as a needle and strong grasses as thread to construct a garment from animal skins. A needle and a single thread have continued to be the primary tools used in creating needlework.

Women have traditionally spent a great deal of their lives doing embroidery. They used needlework to decorate clothing and to create furnishings for the home. Men have used their talents with needle and thread as a way of earning a living. These traditions have passed from generation to generation.

Many European countries produced needlework for their churches. Early inventories listed textiles as a major part of household furnishings. In medieval times, it was customary for the nobility to include their embroidered items when transporting furnishings from one castle or manor home to another when making the rounds of their many estates. In later centuries, men and women used a more secular style of needlework as an art form. Embroidered possessions were not only for comfort; they were a manner in which to display wealth and family pride. For the early American woman, embroidery was an acceptable outlet for creative expression and perhaps her most meaningful contribution to the decorative arts.

This book will focus on a small segment of needlework's history—16th-century English to 19th-century American embroidery. It is these designs of historical needlework that have been interpreted here in 1:12 scale especially for the miniaturist. The designs are a study of the style of original antique needlework rather than a study of technique. Needleworkers will find, among the variety of patterns included in the project sections, exactly the right piece for both their abilities and for the rooms they are planning to reproduce. The collector will be given an overview of the various styles of needlework that have been used through the years and the historical information needed to choose the most authentic designs for their period room furnishing.

Early Needlework
(13th-15th Centuries)

The earliest and oldest and longest has still the mastery of us.
—George Elliot (1819-1880)

The Bayeux Tapestry-11th Century

Photo by special permission of The City of Bayeux

In *The Needleworker's Dictionary*, Pamela Clabburn defines embroidery as "the art of ornamenting material with needlework." Throughout the history of needlework, embroidery has served both as a social and economic activity, but the earliest needlework was done for practical reasons. Primitive man used stitchery to provide clothing for warmth. From this humble beginning, an art form was born.

Adolph S. Cavallo in *Needlework* writes, "Egypt's climate and burial customs worked hand-in-hand to preserve what are the oldest embroideries we know of today, now in the Cairo Museum." These decorative fragments are from the tombs of the pharaoh Thutmose IV (c.1419-1386 B.C.) and the boy king Tutankhamun (1334-1325

B.C.). Cavallo further states, "The embroidery associated with Thutmose IV shows pink and green rosettes worked in satin stitches, all in linen yarns. A tunic from Tutankhamun's tomb has needlework bordering the neckline, the sides and the bottom; the pattern features exquisitely drawn flowers, animals and sphinxes."

The Bible refers to needlework in the book of Exodus. God has instructed Moses to erect a tabernacle or tent and the description for the opening is found in chapter 26, verse 36: "And thou shalt make a hanging for the door of the tent, of blue and purple, and scarlet stuff and fine twined linen, wrought with needlework." Chapter 35, verses 25 and 35 also refer to needlework. Fragments of Indian and Greek embroideries from the 5th century B.C. have survived as have pieces from the frozen tombs of Russia.

The oldest existing European embroidery is a fragment of vestments dated about A.D. 850 at Maasiek, Belgium. In 1827 other vestments were discovered in the tomb of St. Cuthbert in Durham Cathedral in Durham, England. One was a stole, a long narrow band worn by priests; the other was a maniple, which is a shorter strip of material worn by a priest over his left forearm. They were dated about 909-16. In *The Royal School of Needlework Book of Needlework and Embroidery*, edited by Lanto Synge, Rosemary Ewles writes, "Inscriptions incorporated into the design record that they were commissioned by Aelfflaed, the wife of Edward the Elder, for use by Bishop Frithstan of Winchester." Embroidered over the surface of the fabric were figures of saints and prophets.

The best-known vintage embroidery to have survived is the *Bayeux Tapestry* (page 11), which is in the Museum of the Cathedral of Bayeux, France. Commissioned by William the Conqueror's brother, Ode, and made about A.D. 1070-80, the embroidery illustrates the Norman victory over England. The wall hanging is worked on linen with colored wool yarns using the outline stitch. It is about 230 feet wide and 20 inches high. The design is bold in scale, not as delicate as the Durham embroidery, but suitable to the large size of the fabric.

During the 13th and 14th centuries, England produced many ecclesiastical vestments that were collectively known as *Opus Anglicanum*, Latin for *English work*. The work was regarded as the most exquisite in design and was sought by churches throughout Europe. A 1295 inventory showed that the Vatican had more English needlework than any other country. Most pieces were designed by artistically talented monks and embroidered by male professionals, although some were stitched by nuns. The exceptional workmanship, using colored silks on the finest materials (silk, taffeta, satin), revealed stitches so fine that much detail could be achieved in facial expressions. Another technique called *couching* was used with gold and silver thread. One thread was laid on top of the fabric and attached by an additional thread sewn over it.

The full-size *Syon Cope* is in the collection of the Victoria and Albert Museum in London.

The embroidered designs on copes were usually scenes from the Bible. A cope was an outer garment resembling a cloak in its shape and design. It was worn by officials of the church on special occasions. The *Syon Cope* at the Victoria and Albert Museum in London portrays scenes from the life of Christ. The figures fan outward from the central motif. The framework was like that of stained glass, different scenes arranged in connecting compartments. The *Jesse Cope*, also at the Victoria and Albert Museum, is embroidered on a red silk twill ground. It portrays the Old Testament Jesse and his descendants linked by circles of vine branches.

Professional embroiderers produced other items for secular use. They were commissioned by the royalty and nobility to make costumes, clothing,

Detail of the full-size *Syon Cope*.

Photos courtesy of V & A Picture Gallery

furnishings, horse trappings, tents and banners. In *Antique Needlework*, Lanto Synge states, "Even the Squire who went on the Canterbury pilgrimage was attired in needle-work according to Chaucer:

> Embrouded was he, as it were a mede
>
> Al, ful of freshe floures whyte and rede.

Very few secular items from this period have survived because they were used often and eventually wore out.

The decline of *Opus Anglicanum* came in the middle of the 14th century. Causes were the Black Death—an epidemic of bubonic plague that devastated Europe from 1346 to 1353—and the economic problems created by the Hundred Years War with France (1337-1453). Interest in embroidering heraldic subjects on banners, horse trappings, clothing and household items became more desirable and admirable. Using heraldry as acknowledgement of family status was considered a privilege of birth.

The troubled and unsettled 15th century affected artists and craftsmen, and the quality of their work. Stitchery during this period was still elaborate, but lacked the fineness seen in earlier works.

Chapter 1

16th-Century
English Needlework

Perfection is attained by slow degrees; it requires the hand of time.
—Francis M. Voltaire (1694-1778)

Following the *Opus-Anglicanum* period, 16th-century embroidery in England became known for its uniqueness. So unlike the work of the same period in other countries, it blossomed into an art form due to the creativity and talents of the individual stitchers. The Elizabethan period brought a more innovative and domesticated style of embroidery. Designs were almost entirely secular and usually worked by amateurs, often guided by professionals.

A more gracious way of living evolved after the Reformation, the religious movement in 16th-century Europe that led to the break with the Church of Rome. A new prosperous society emerged, resulting in the building of more comfortable and splendid manor homes. England settled into a period of cultural growth and the new middle class began to give more attention to the decor of their homes and dress, often imitating the riches enjoyed by the nobility. Successful tradesmen and merchants boasted of their new wealth by their displays of luxuries, which almost always included embroidered items. It was the ladies of the household who used their needles to create most of the decorative clothing and household furnishings. Since England was ruled by women from 1553 to 1603, there seemed to be a greater interest in the decorative arts.

Queen Elizabeth I (1533-1603) received an extensive education, including instruction in needlework. Among the several items worked by her that still exist are baby linens made for her half-sister, Mary. She gave her step-mother, Queen Katherine Parr, book bindings for *Mirroir or Glasse of the Synnefull Soule*, a manuscript translated by Elizabeth herself, and bindings for a set of Pauline Epistles. Due to Elizabeth's appreciation of the needle arts, many of the finest embroideries were produced during her reign.

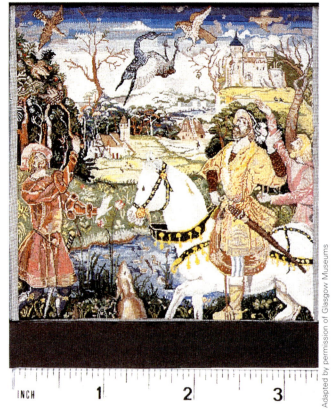

Adapted by permission of Glasgow Museums

Daphne Turner needlework: *Flight of the Heron*, stitched by Daphne in tent stitch on #84 silk gauze. The miniature was adapted from an already reduced photograph of a Franco-Netherlandish tapestry of about 1515, which probably shows Francis I of France hawking.

The flight of a peregrine against a heron—three times its own weight—was a frequent subject for tapestries. The birds include doves, a kestrel, mallards with chicks and a jack snipe, as well as the peregrine and the heron. Flowers are tulip, bulrush, primula and wild cyclamen leaves. Actual size: 3½ in. x 3¼ in.

Professional embroiderers still existed in England, but their trade had become more specialized. The Broderer's Company workshops were incorporated in October 1561, and were mostly responsible for ceremonial embroidery. In many instances, professional and amateur needleworkers worked together. Often a noble household would employ a professional embroiderer, and not necessarily a Broderer Company member, to teach designing or to draw the design on the canvas for the amateur needleworker. This practice by no means took away from the creativity of the amateur. No doubt the larger household furnishings were done by the professional and the smaller furnishings were stitched by the lady of the house. In the last half of the 16th century, during the reign of Elizabeth I and the literary achievements of William Shakespeare, decorative arts reached new heights in skill and originality.

At a time when there was a limited supply of pattern books, the best way to preserve a favorite pattern was to take a piece of cloth and reproduce that pattern on it. In *Antique Needlework*, Lanto Synge writes: "There is evidence in records and inventories to show that samplers were worked extensively in the 16th century. These take their name from the French *essamplaire* and Latin *exemplarium* meaning *example*, and consisted of small lengths of cloths on which were recorded examples of stitches, border patterns and motifs."

The various motifs of animals or birds and flowers, and perhaps geometric patterns, were usually scattered at random on the small pieces of cloth and used as a means for experimenting with designs. These "records" were kept by adult women, rolled and put away when not in use. Mr. Synge in *Antique Needlework* refers to the Barnabe Riche story, "Of Phylotus and Emilia" (1581), in describing the activities of a wealthy wife:

> Now, when she had dined, then she might seke out her examplers, and to peruse whiche worke would doe beste in a ruffe, whiche in a gorget, whiche in a sleeve, whiche in a quaife, which in a caule, whiche in a handercheef; what lace would doe beste to edge it, what seame, what stitch, what cutte, what garde: and to sitte her doune and take it forthe by little and little, and thus with her nedle to passe the after noone with devising of thinges for her owne wearynge.

The earliest English sampler in existence is dated 1598 and was made by Jane Bostocke. Now in the Victoria and Albert Museum, London, it is detailed with a variety of stitches and spot motifs of several animals and flowers, followed by an alphabet and an inscription to the two-year-old Alice Lee. These samples of stitches and patterns were necessary reference tools for the skilled embroiderer for use in the decorating of costumes and household furnishings.

However, there is written evidence of an earlier sampler in the 1502 account book of Queen Elizabeth of York. Marguerite Fawdry and Deborah Brown in *The Book of Samplers* say the will of Margaret Thomson made in 1546 at Freston in Holland, Lincolnshire, states, "I gyve to Alys Pynchebeck my sisters daughter my sawmpler with semes."

Small (1 in. x 1 in.) field of flowers taken from the background of a medieval tapestry. Stitched by Daphne Turner on #112 silk gauze. Sarah Salisbury Collection.

Photo by Jason Getzan

Favorite subjects of Elizabethan embroidery were flowers, herbs, insects and wild animals.

Inspiration for the many designs and motifs could be found in the lavish English garden. Often the needleworker referred to herbals and bestiaries as sources. Projects were found in pattern books of embroidery designs that were first published in Germany in 1524, then later published by France and Italy.

In 16th-century England, embroidery was done for a purpose, even if the lavishness outweighed the need. Inventories from the great houses are filled with references to embroidered hangings and cushions. Velvet and satin were often used as ground fabric, as was damask and linen. These materials were usually imported, and very expensive. After the Reformation, the fine silk and velvet materials once used for the church vestments were acquired by private homes and used for hangings, cushions and coverlets. However, the tent stitch on linen canvas was the most popular and widely used combination of technique and material for the majority of the household furnishings.

Tudor Bedroom. Room, carving, and furniture by Tom Warner. Needlepoint table carpet by Annelle Ferguson, upholstery by Frank Hanley and Jeffery Gueno, embroidery box and gold jewel box by William R. Robertson. Collection of the Toy and Miniature Museum of Kansas City.

Photo courtesy of Toy and Miniature Museum of Kansas City

A favorite method for decorating bed hangings and cushions used what was called appliquèd *slips*. Small motifs taken from the various reference and pattern books were individually stitched on a linen canvas. After reaching the required number of motifs needed for a specific project, each was cut out and attached onto another material such as velvet or satin. This was appealing to the needleworker since it was easier to decorate with small motifs worked separately than to embroider directly on the ground fabric. For a finished appearance, the edges were couched with colorful threads. The famous Oxburgh bed hangings, Oxburgh Hall, Norfolk,—attributed to Mary Queen of Scots and Bess of Hardwick—are exceptional examples of applied work. The slips were worked in tent stitch, using colored silk thread on a linen canvas and then attached to a rich green velvet background fabric.

The bedroom was usually furnished more elaborately than any other room in the house during this period. Heavily embroidered bed hangings not only provided warmth and privacy, but exhibited the wealth of the household. The professional embroiderer is given credit for the more detailed overall needleworked hangings. The designs often resembled the intricate tapestries in vogue at that time.

Embroidered coverlets, or counterpanes, have not survived as well as the bed hangings. Being used daily, they eventually wore out, and were sometimes cut up to be used in another form. The pattern of one surviving bed cover is described as having all-over scrolling stems with flowers and leaves. Pillow covers, also known as *pillow beres*, were additional luxuries made for the bed. They were often the same size as large cushions but were always worked on a white linen ground with silk threads. The patterns were usually florals in a continuous spiraling form. Several of the finest examples of Elizabethan blackwork, embroidery with black silk thread on linen fabric, are found on existing pillow covers. The Victoria and Albert Museum in London has one such example.

The living rooms of the manor homes had very little furniture. There were a few tables and perhaps a cupboard. Chairs were reserved for the head of the household and his wife. Benches and stools were for other members of the family or guests. Cushions were a necessity to soften the hard wooden seats. Embroidered cushions were yet another symbol of prosperity, and added greatly to the decor of the room. Some were made of velvet with applied embroidery slips. Often the cushions were embroidered on linen canvas with floral and symmetrical designs. The Tudor rose was a favorite subject for the smaller, squared cushions. Longer cushions might have had pastoral scenes that told a story, often themes from mythology or the Bible.

Four slips: Dog Rose, Pansy, Starflower, Peaseblossom. Project 1A, 1B, 1C, 1D.

Carpets in the 16th century were placed on tables or cupboards rather than on the floor. The knotted pile carpets were imported from Turkey and were considered a luxury in the European home. It is probable that the more detailed embroidered carpets, worked on canvas in tent stitch, were made professionally.

The Victoria and Albert Museum, London, has two exceptional examples, the Gifford and Bradford table carpets. The Gifford carpet, dated about 1550, is very long and narrow, eighteen feet long by four feet, eight inches wide. The design is basically geometric with three roundels set in the field, each encircled by a wreath of flowers. The center roundel contains the Gifford arms and the other two show a pastoral scene with a stag sitting under a tree. The Bradford carpet dates from the late 16th century and is also long and narrow. The field pattern is a trellis with an intertwining grapevine. The border, which is 17 inches in depth and hangs over the edge of the table, is stitched with scenes of rural life with a pastoral landscape.

Counted thread embroidery was used frequently for other household furnish-

Top

Elizabethan blackwork pillow cover. Project 4.

ings. Embroidery on linen or velvet was commonly used for book bindings. A considerable number exist and are thought to be primarily worked by professionals. The usual subject matter was Tudor roses or coats of arms, beautifully created with silk and metal threads.

Costumes reached a peak of excellence in the decades from 1540 to 1600. Portraits from the Elizabethan period show exquisite floral designs on formal clothing worn by Queen Elizabeth I and by men and women of the nobility. Amateur embroidery was done on small articles such as jackets and waistcoats, caps, hoods and scarves. The more elaborate designs were embroidered by professionals. Any article of clothing could be decorated with embroidery, very often including jewels attached with gold threads.

The aforementioned blackwork was a popular form of decoration and already fashionable during the reign of Henry VIII. The introduction of this style of embroidery

Elizabethan seat cushion. Project 2.

Book cover. Project 3.

to England was once attributed to Catherine of Aragon but the technique was known before her 1501 arrival from Spain. By Elizabeth's reign, blackwork, also known as Spanish work, was used on both costumes and household furnishings.

A variety of motifs was used in blackwork. Coiling stems and leaves was a favorite design usually found on collars and sleeves of court dress. A double running stitch, meaning the pattern was worked to create identical designs on both sides of the fabric, was often used. This technique was used mostly for collars and cuffs where both sides were exposed.

Gloves were an essential arti-

Photo by Peter Charman

Queen Elizabeth doll, needleworked costume by Ann Crompton.

Photo by Ivan Turner

A white kit 16th-century guantlet glove by Daphne Turner lies on a 3½-inch square table by Ivan Turner. The inlaid table replicates one from Hardwick Hall, home of Bess of Hardwick. A roll of lute music is in the handwriting of composer John Dowland.

cle of court dress. Known as gauntlets, they were originally worn with medieval armor. In the Elizabethan period, gauntlets were described as the part that attached to the glove and flared out from the wrist. The glove itself was made of leather, whereas the design of the gauntlet was elegantly embroidered on silk and applied to the leather. Gloves, which were often scented and given as gifts, were made professionally.

Inventories list *sweet bags* as New Year's gifts frequently given to Queen Elizabeth. They were small purses measuring about four inches by three inches. Many survive. They were professionally embroidered with floral patterns worked with gold, silver and colorful silk threads on a linen canvas. Most had plaited drawstrings of silk thread and were lined with satin or taffeta. They were commonly used for carrying candies or sweet-smelling herbs. These small bags are considered among the most decorative examples of 16th-century embroidery.

Perhaps the most famous Elizabethan needlework was done by Mary Queen of Scots. Mary Stuart (1542-1587), became Queen of Scotland upon the death of her father, James V, when only a few weeks old. She was sent to France at an early age and placed under the guardianship of the French court. Her broad education included the fine art of embroidery. As most of her life was plagued by political discord, her stitchery skill became a source of pleasure for her.

Six years after her return to Scotland, Mary was taken prisoner. A portion of her years in custody was spent in the company of Elizabeth Shrewsbury, known as Bess of Hardwick. Together, they created a series of medallions portraying emblems, plants, exotic birds and beasts, and plants. It was thought that a professional embroiderer may have drawn the designs on the canvas, adapting them from woodcut illustrations. The designs, attached to a velvet ground, eventually became known as the previously mentioned Oxburgh hangings. During the years of her captivity, Mary often attempted to entice Queen Elizabeth with gifts of embroidery.

During most of the 16th century, the interests of the times usually centered on the activities of the court. Records show that all ladies of high birth used their leisure time to create beautiful embroidery. The love for fine furnishings and decorative costumes continued throughout the Stuart monarchy.

Full-size *Oxburgh Hangings*, Victoria and Albert Museum. Velvet hanging with applied slips of canvas work, last quarter of 16th century.

Photo T291955, VAS276 used with permission, V & A Picture Library

16th-Century English Needlework

All projects are for personal use only. They may not be stitched and sold for profit.

PROJECT #1.1A
Pansy (Slips)
Designed by: Ann Crompton

Materials Needed:
 #72 silk gauze
 Silk sewing thread/embroidery floss

Stitch Count:
 60 (w) x 80 (h)
 Approx. finished size: ⅚ in. x 1⅛ in.

Color Chart:

Code	Color	Comparable to DMC #'s
●	Black	310
○	Lt. Blue	809
▼	Dk. Violet	3746
◿	Plum	917
│	Lt. Moss Green	3819
c	Dk. Canary	972
·	Golden Yellow	3078
✕	Emerald Green	911
⊙	Blue Green	500
☐	Ecru (Background)	

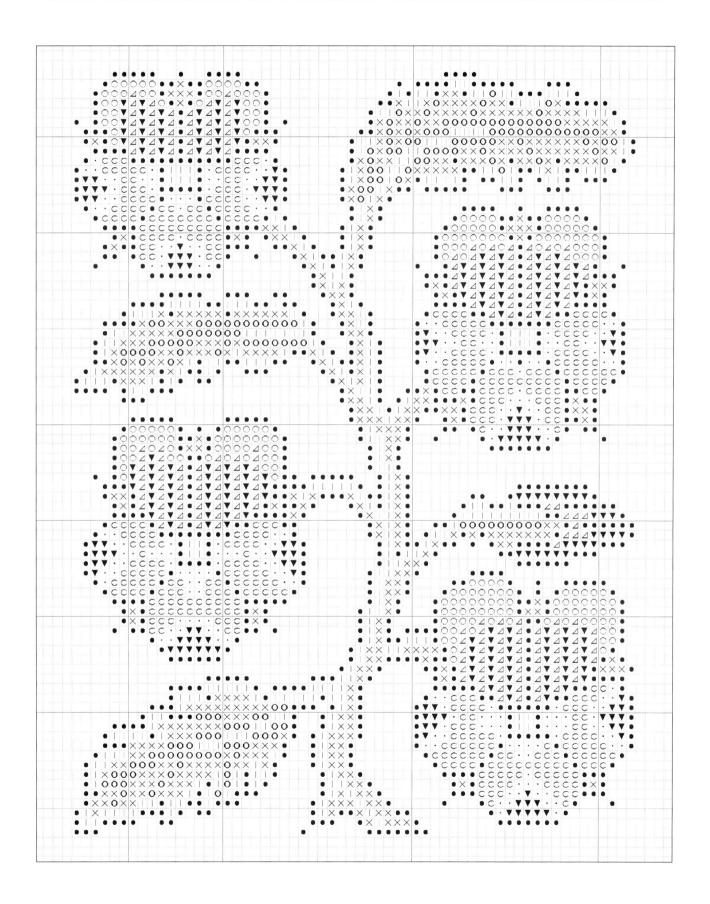

PROJECT #1.1B
Starflower (Slips)
Designed by: Ann Crompton

Materials Needed:
> #72 silk gauze
> Silk sewing thread/embroidery floss

Stitch Count:
> 60 (w) x 80 (h)
> Approx. finished size: 5/6 in. x 1 1/8 in.

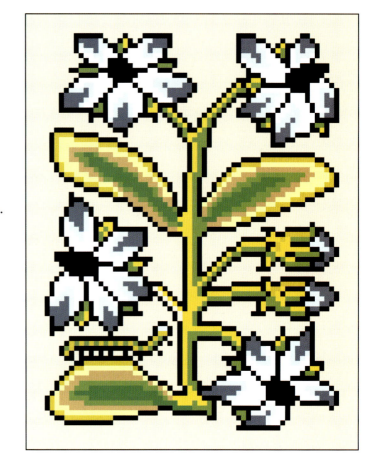

Color Chart:

Code	Color	Comparable to DMC #'s
●	Black	310
✕	Dk. Blue	824
◿	Med. Blue	827
·	Lt. Blue	3756
▼	Dk. Emerald Green	3818
△	Lt. Moss Green	3819
○	Chartreuse	703
+	Lt. Olive Green	734
▮	Dk. Lemon	444
−	Pale Yellow	744
□	Ecru	

PROJECT #1.1C
Pease Blossom (Slip)
Designed by: Ann Crompton

Materials Needed:
> #72 silk gauze
> Silk sewing thread/embroidery floss

Stitch Count:
> 60 (w) x 78 (h)
> Approx. finished size: ⁵⁄₆ in. x 1¹⁄₈ in.

Color Chart:

Code	Color	Comparable to DMC #'s
●	Black	310
╱	Lt. Rose	3326
○	Med. Mauve	316
◢	Dk. Mauve	3803
○	Dk. Emerald Green	3818
▼	Med. Dk. Emerald Green	909
➤	Med. Emerald Green	911
△	Lt. Emerald Green	912
✖	Dk. Parrot Green	905
+	Moss Green	581
		Lt. Olive Green	734
·	Lt. Jade Green	564
−	Topaz	725
□	Ecru (Background)	

PROJECT #1.1D
Dog Rose (Slips)
Designed by: Ann Crompton

Materials Needed:
> #72 silk gauze
> Silk sewing thread/embroidery floss

Stitch Count:
> 90 (w) x 90 (h)
> Approx. finished size: 1¼ in. x 1¼ in.

Color Chart:

Code	Color	Comparable to DMC #'s
●	Black	310
◢	Rose	335
—	Carnation	893
·	Pink	776
○	Topaz	725
❙	Lemon	307
+	Lt. Lemon	445
✕	Dk. Brown	611
≡	Lt. Brown	613
❘	Med. Beige Grey	644
▼	Christmas Red	321
△	Lt. Mahogany	402
▲	Chartreuse	703
▽	Hazelnut Brown	3828
○	Dk. Pistachio	319
∨	Lt. Moss Green	3819
□	Ecru (Background)	

PROJECT #1.2
Elizabethan Seat Cushion
Designed by: Annelle Ferguson

Materials Needed:
    #48 silk gauze
    DMC embroidery floss

Stitch Count:
    47 (h) x 69 (w)
    Approx. finished size 1 in. x 1¹/₂ in.

Color Chart:

Code	Color	Comparable to DMC #'s
✘	Red	347
•	Peach	3712
╱	Off-White	746
○	Pine Green	320
□	Navy (background)	823

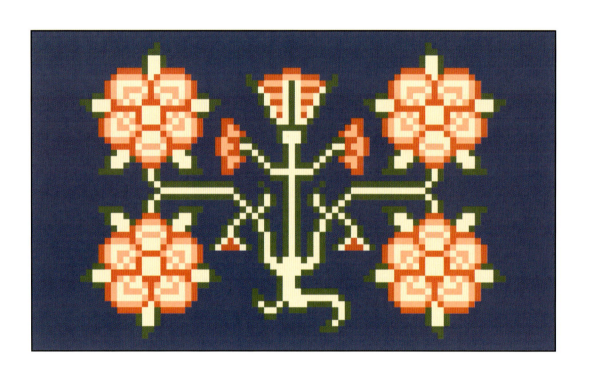

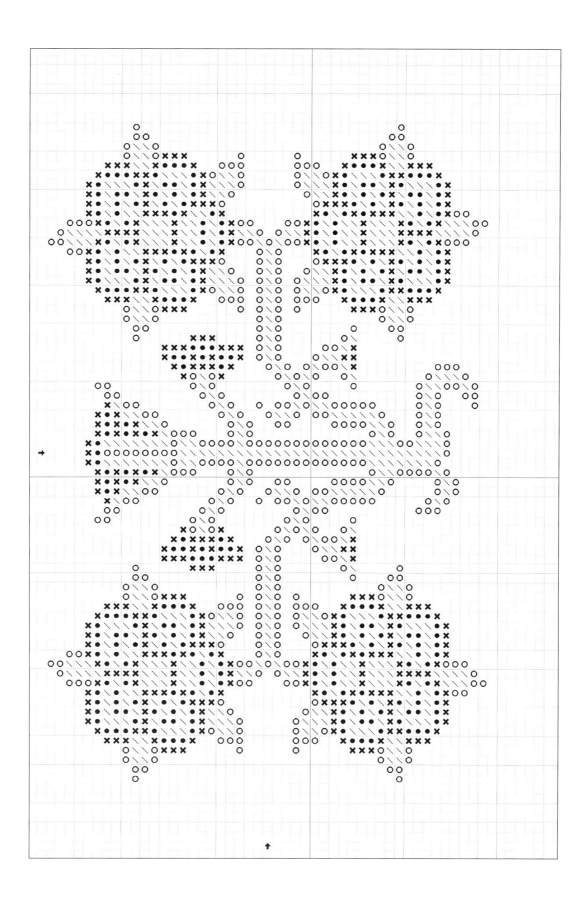

PROJECT #1.3
Book Cover
Designed by: Annelle Ferguson

Materials Needed:
>   #56 silk gauze
>   Silk sewing thread/embroidery floss

Stitch Count:
>   65(w) x 61(h)
>   Approx. finished size: 1 in. x 7/8 in.

Special Instructions:
>   Reverse pattern for back cover.

Color Chart:

Code	Color	Comparable to DMC #'s
I	Dk. Green	319
•	Med. Green	367
o	Lt. Green	320
R	Pale Green	369
✖	Dk. Rust	347
▼	Med. Rust	3385
S	Med. Peach	760
V	Lt. Peach	3713
▲	Dk. Gold	741
Z	Med. Gold	743
C	Lt. Gold	746
✚	Dk. Blue	930
B	Med. Blue	931
L	Lt. Blue	3753
➤	Brown	420
□	Off-White (Background)	543

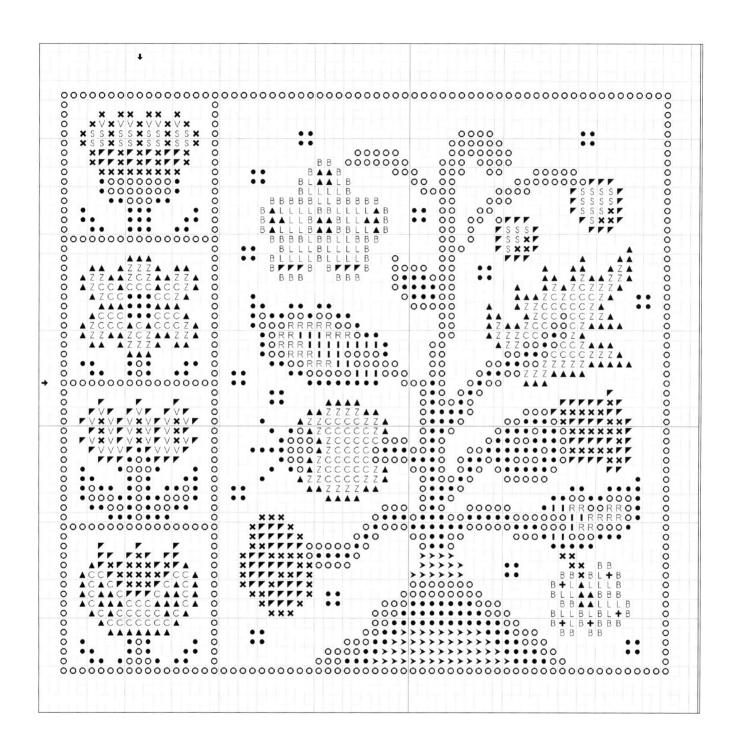

PROJECT #1.4
Blackwork Pillow Cover
Designed by: Jessie Harrison

Materials Needed:
> #32 Jobelan linen
> *(Smaller count even weave linen may be substituted)*
> Black silk thread
> Approx. finished size: 3¼ in. x 2¼ in.

DIRECTIONS:

——————— Backstitch using one strand of black silk thread.
——————— Backstitch using two strands of black silk thread

Chapter 2

17th-Century
English Needlework

The purest of pleasures lie within the circle of useful occupation.
—Henry Ward Beecher (1813-1887)

The long reign of Elizabeth I ended in 1603. At last, Scotland and England were united when James I, son of Mary Stuart, ascended the throne. The Elizabethan style of embroidery continued its popularity throughout the first half of the century. During the decades that linked the Tudor and Stuart dynasties, domestic embroidery was at its best.

The Stuarts ruled Great Britain from 1603 until the death of Queen Anne in 1714. James I was on the throne from 1605 to 1625. Charles I (1625-1649) ascended the throne upon the death of his father. After Charles's overthrow, the Puritan Commonwealth, under the leadership of Oliver Cromwell, ruled England until 1660. Creative embroidery was not adversely affected during these turbulent times, but the gaiety of it seemed to have disappeared. The Restoration began with the return of Charles II to England from France, after Cromwell's death. He reigned until 1685.

Interest in needlework was revived and there was an outpouring of fancy embroidery created during the Restoration. James II (1685-88) gave up the throne and it was offered to his daughter, Mary, and her husband, William of Orange. William and Mary (1689-1702) sat on the throne for the final decade of the century. Mary herself had an absorbing interest in embroidery and spent many hours a day on her work. A queen who embroidered was an unusual sight to members of her court.

Under the influence of Elizabethan embroidery, early-17th-century needlework became richer with the use of silver and gold threads. Blackwork fell from favor, but many of its distinctive elements later appeared in crewelwork. Fashions saw little change at the beginning of the century. By mid-century, costumes were more lavish and ornate, but not extravagant. Embroiderers continued to use the same materials. Canvas remained the fabric most used for furnishings such as cushions. Embroiderers also continued to apply slips to satin and velvet.

Embroidery resumed its importance for wall and bed hangings, prominent features in middle-class households. Needleworked book covers, bags and purses remained popular. The Bible was translated into English in 1611 and was therefore available to the common people. Many embroidered Bible covers from the 17th century still exist today. Table carpets remained fashionable household furnishings throughout the first half of the century. Imported knotted carpets were expensive and not affordable for most middle-class families. Professional workshops created, in canvas work, direct imitations of the Eastern designs and other carpets in the typical designs of the period. By late in the century, table carpets were replaced by floor carpets. Early-17th-century embroidery flourished and blossomed as it became bolder and more exotic in design.

Bedhangings in miniature by Rosemary Conway-Jones, England. Bargello design worked on #72 silk gauze, using silk threads. The design was adapted from the curtains on the bed in the Great Chamber at Parham Park, Sussex, UK. The original curtains are dated c. 1615 and are worked in Hungarian point in a flame design. The 1:12 scale bed was made by Barry Hipwell.

Close-up of flame-stitched bed hangings.

Table carpet, designed by Lucy Iducovich. Gateleg table and chair by Gerald Crawford. Candlestick by Emily Good. Project 2.1.

Band sampler designed by Pat Tulski. Project 2.2. Sampler framed by Margaret Nine using SH Goode molding. Wing chair flame stitch upholstery designed by Martha (Stubby) Crowe, chair designed and upholstered by Donna Johnson. Project 2.6.

A great deal of the needlework was produced in professional workshops, but the skills mastered by the amateurs displayed their discipline and training in the art of embroidery. It was customary for mothers to teach their daughters all the accomplishments they themselves had learned as children.

Samplers reached a peak of excellence in 17th-century England. Referred to as *band samplers* they were worked on long narrow strips of linen six to eight inches wide and often as much as 24 inches in length. The designs were bands of border patterns worked with colored threads. The patterns continued to be used as references for decorating clothing and household furnishings. The material most often used for samplers was a fine, even-weave linen. The required size could be woven on a loom kept in the home. Cut work and drawn work were sometimes incorporated into the piece in the first half of the century.

By midcentury, samplers were worked as part of a young girl's education. Conquering the more elaborate patterns with precise detail was included as a technical exercise in their school curriculum. After 1650, alphabets and numerals, the name of the maker and the date of the work were included as well as religious and moral verses. By the second half of the century, samplers ceased to be a reference tool for patterns.

Books containing patterns and designs drawn specifically for the needleworker to copy were being published in the 17th century. At a time when there were no copyright laws, publishers often copied patterns from each other. *The Schole House of the Needle* by Richard Shorleyker was published in 1624. In *Samplers, Five Centuries of a Gentle Craft*, Anne Sebba writes that Shorleyker declared his book contained:

> Certaine Patternes of Cut-workes: newly invented and never published
> before. Also sundry sortes of spots as Flowers, Birdes and fishes, etc. and
> will fitly serve to be wrought some with gould, some with silke, some with
> crewell in coullers: or otherwise at your pleasure.

In 1630, Thomas Johnson's imaginative title, *A Book of Beasts, Birds, Flowers, Fruits, Flies, and Worms, exactly drawn with their Lively Colours truly Described*, contained drawings of engravings from English, Dutch and German sources. Another popular pattern book was *The Needle's Excellency*, published by James Boler in 1631. Many such publications appeared throughout the century to provide the embroiderer patterns for small and large creatures, fruits and flowers. Other inspiring sources were books on gardening, animals, heraldry and the Bible, the same as used in the previous century.

Popular for about 30 years during the middle of the century was raised work. By padding and stuffing many parts of the design, a high relief was achieved. Designs were drawn on satin, silk, or canvas. The flat details were stitched on the background material first. The raised figures were constructed separately, padded with cotton or hair, and then attached to the background material. Occasionally the needleworker would paint on facial features.

The main themes of the embroidered designs derived from prints or engravings of biblical, classical and allegorical scenes. Historical or biblical characters would be interacting with animals, insects, birds, plants and flowers in landscape settings.

This form of needlework was found on small cabinets or caskets, mirror frames and pictures. Caskets were box-shaped cabinets with a flat or domed lid, two doors in front that opened to a nest of drawers, many having a secret compartment in back. The inside of the lid usually held a mirror and the surface was used to store ink bottles, sewing implements and various other objects treasured by the owner. The drawers, lined in silk or colored paper, were for rings or coins or special trinkets. The four ball-feet were made of wood or metal. These elaborately decorated cabinets were placed on a table or dressing table in the maker's bedchamber.

Upon completion of a band sampler and a cut-and-drawn whitework sampler, a young girl, often a teenager, might proceed to doing small embroidered panels to be placed on a casket. The completed panels, for all four sides and the lid, were sent to a cabinetmaker for mounting. The panels were cut to size and glued to the wooden frame, which was constructed to fit the needlework, then trimmed with braid or ribbon, or edged with a tortoise-shell border.

Photo by Kevin Housley, courtesy of the Toy and Miniature Museum of Kansas City

Casket, built and designed by William R. Robertson, needlework covering of various scenes of elegantly dressed English gentlemen and ladies stitched on #60 silk gauze by Esther Robertson. Project 2.3. Mirror surround designed and stitched on #60 silk gauze by Annelle Ferguson. Scene of King and Queen surrounded by domestic and wild animals. Inner frame of polished tortoise-shell and outer molding of wavy boxwood designed by William R. Robertson. Nickel was used for the mirror giving a rippling effect much like antique mirrors. The table and chair on the opening page of this chapter are by David Hurley. Candlestick by William R. Robertson.

Margaret Fawdry and Deborah Brown, in *The Book of Sampler*, recognize Hannah Smith and her account of the completion of her panels for her casket. Hannah's note was found inside the box which is now in the collection of the Whitworth Art Gallery, Manchester, England:

> the yere of Our Lord being 1657.
> if ever I have any thoughts about the time when I went to Oxford, as it may be I may, when I have forgoten the time, to sartifi myself I may loock in this paper and find it; I went to Oxford in the yere of 1654 and my being thare near 2 years, for I went in 1654, and I stayed there 1655 and I cam away in 1656; and I was allmost 12 yers of age when I went, and I mad an end of my cabbinet at Oxford...and my cabbinet was mad up in the yere of 1656 at London. I have written this to sattisfi myself and thos that shall inquir about it. Hannah Smith.

International Guild of Miniature Artisians Medieval Period Clock Case, designed by Le Chateau Interiors. Needlework mirror surround designed and stitched by Annelle Ferguson. Featuring other works by George and Sally Hoffman, Lee Ann Chellis-Wessell, Willian R. Robertson, Le Chateau Interiors, Don Shaw and William T. Whiting. From the Cookie Ziemba collection. (*Miniature Collector*, Spring, 1994, p. 21)

Embroidered mirror frames were another means of displaying female talent. As mirrors were expensive and usually small, the table and wall mirrors needed to be surrounded with a frame to enlarge and protect them. The same techniques were applied as on the embroidered panels for caskets. The mirror itself was framed with walnut or tortoise shell, then placed within the embroidered frame, which was then given an outer frame of the same materials as the inner frame.

Subject matters on caskets and mirror frames were usually Old Testament themes. During the Commonwealth, the Puritans frowned upon embroidered scenes from the life of Christ or any other New Testament setting, but the same techniques and themes have been found on canvas-worked pictorial embroidery popular during the middle of the century.

Large wall hangings were being replaced by wood paneling in fashionable homes in mid-century, so 17th-century embroidered pictures were meant to be framed and hung on the wall. Paneled walls of dark wood provided a desirable backdrop for the colorful stitchery. Most were worked in tent stitch on linen canvas. The same scenes and motifs appear on so many pictures that it is believed canvases could be obtained with patterns already drawn out.

Biblical figures such as David and Bathsheba, Solomon and the Queen of Sheba and

Abraham and the angels were popular subjects. The figures were often standing on a landscaped area and were surrounded by large and small animals, birds, flowers and trees, usually without regard to proportion. The sun and the moon were frequently placed among the clouds. Additional themes represented the four seasons and the five senses, while other designs were linked to the Stuarts.

In middle-class households, embroidery continued to be an important feature for bed hangings. Early in the reign of James I, a new style developed. It was based on the coiling stems and flower designs of Elizabethan blackwork. The patterns were enlarged and rendered in colorful wool yarns called *crewel*. (The term *crewel* meant a worsted yarn of two threads used specifically for embroidery. It did not identify the *style* of embroidery.)

Crewelwork was produced both at home by the amateur and in workshops by professionals. The fabric was a new blend of cotton and linen twill embroidered with crewel wool. Crewel embroidery became an enjoyable pursuit for women just as raised work was for their children. The overall pattern of large meandering stems and bold floral patterns was repeated over the entire fabric to create bed hangings and valances.

Full-size 17th-century embroidered picture. Debbie Slone collection, Bloomfield Village, Michigan.

Adam and Eve seat cushion designed and stitched by Corky Anderson. Various motifs taken from 17th- and 18th-century styles.

In the first quarter of the century, foreign trade throughout Europe had exposed the English to different art styles. Embroiderers were particularly impressed with goods imported from China and India. During the reign of Charles I, a new style of crewel embroidery was developed by the blending of East and West influences. From the English embroiderers' love of the countryside, the famous Tree-of-Life design evolved. In *The Needleworker's Dictionary*, Pamela Clabburn says, "The designs often consisted of large leaves and flowers springing from a tree trunk, generally with small hills or hummocks at the base on which might be stags, rabbits, squirrels, etc." The bed sets included curtains, valances, pillows and bed covers, all embroidered with individual but coordinating designs.

Another change occurred in designs for crewel bed hangings before the end of the century. The patterns were bolder, with more exotic branches or with trees growing from mounds and

Photo by Peter Charman

Seventeenth-century chair (c. 1625) by Reg Miller. Upholstery by Rosemary Conway-Jones. Repeat design stitched on #54 silk gauze with silk threads. The inspiration for the design is from an embroidery at the Victoria and Albert Museum, London. Project 2.5.

sprouting elaborate baroque leaves. The designs were a mixture of elements found in Oriental and Western textiles and Flemish tapestries.

Furniture styles changed considerably during the last half of the century. Fully upholstered furniture was introduced in England after the Restoration and needlework became a popular form of covering. A renewed interest in canvas work, using colorful wool and silk threads in tent and cross stitches, surfaced.

Side chairs, stools, settees, sofas, daybeds and wing chairs all became vehicles for decorative canvas work. Already popular in the late 16th century and used extensively in the 17th, was the design of jagged upright stitches called *Florentine*, *Hungarian* or *flame* stitch. The large-scale flame, four or five inches in height, was the favored pattern late in the century. The effect of the design depended on the height of the stitches combined with the shading of the individual bands.

By the end of the 17th century, canvas work was the most commonly used technique for embroidered household furnishings. This particular form of needlework continued in popularity throughout the 18th century.

All projects are for personal use only. They may not be stitched and sold for profit.

PROJECT #2.1
Persian Table Carpet
Designed by: Lucy Iducovich

Materials Needed:
  #40 silk gauze
  DMC embroidery floss

Stitch Count:
  229 (w) x 281 (h)
  Finished size: 5½ in. x 7 in.

Color Chart:

Code	Color	Comparable to DMC #'s
/	Gold	437
●	Navy (Border Background)	939
✖	Dk. Rust (Center ground Background)	355
+	Med. Green	502
○	Lt. Green	503
–	Ecru	

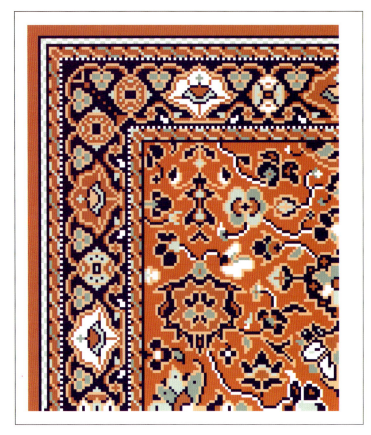

PROJECT #2.2
17th Century Band Sampler
Designed by: Pat Tulski

Materials Needed:
    #48 silk gauze
    DMC embroidery floss

Stitch Count:
    39 (w) x 147 (h)
    Finished size: 1 in. x 3¼ in.

Color Chart:

Code	Color	Comparable to DMC #'s
I	Dk. Green	3051
−	Med. Green	3052
✖	Navy	336
▼	Med. Blue	312
○	Red	815
•	Dk. Gold	832
V	Med. Brown	841
□	Off-White (Background)	543

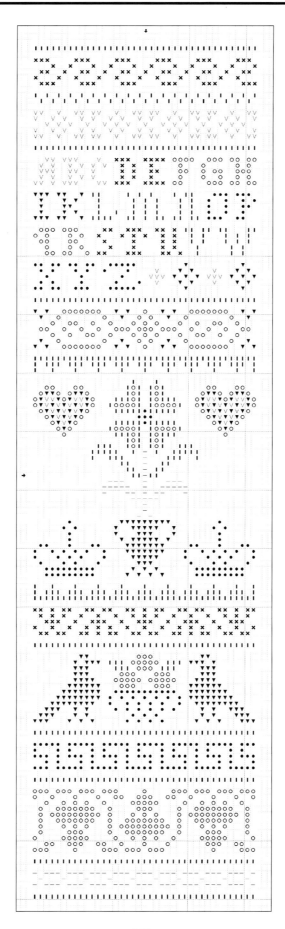

PROJECT #2.3
Casket
Designed by: William R. Robertson
Stitched by: Esther Robertson

Materials Needed:
- #60 silk gauze
- Silk sewing thread/embroidery floss
- Approx. size: 3/4 in. (w) x 3/4 in. (h) x 5/8 in. (d)

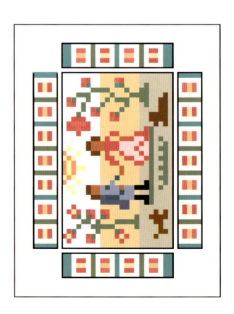

Photo by Kevin Hosley

Color Chart:

Code	Color	Comparable to DMC #'s	Code	Color	Comparable to DMC #'s
o	Dk. Forest Green	367	⏷	Med. Gold	729
L	Lt. Forext Green	368	B	Lt. Gold	676
✕	Deep Rose	3350	■	Navy Blue	311
/	Med. Rose	3731	✛	Med. Navy Blue	312
C	Lt. Rose	3354	V	Med. Blue	334
●	Deep Teal Blue	517	≡	Dk. Copper	922
+	Med. Teal Blue	518	S	Yellow	743
U	Lt. Teal Blue	3761	▲	Dk. Terra Cotta	355
◤	Ult. Dk. Coffee Brown	938	▽	Dk. Salmon	347
≈	Dk. Coffee Brown	801	▼	Black	3799
#	Med. Brown	839	❙	Dk. Grey	646
➤	Lt. Brown	434	Z	Med. Grey	648
T	Lt. Tan	738	W	White	
◢	Dk. Shell Pink	3721	□	Beige	842
F	Flesh	3773			
◖	Dk. Gold	680			

Special Note: Landscape top of lid and top panels and four sides of casket with light forest green, light tan, and light teal blue.

Casket-Lid

Casket-Front

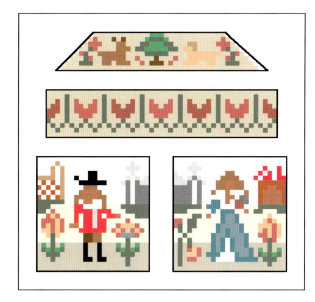

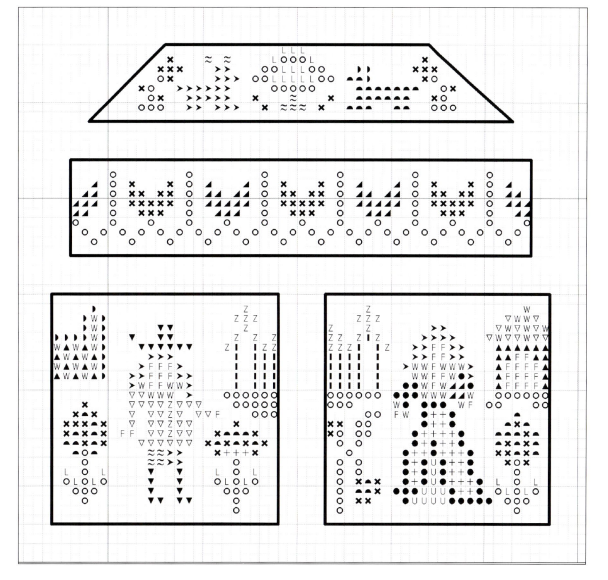

Casket-Back

Photo by Kevin Hosley

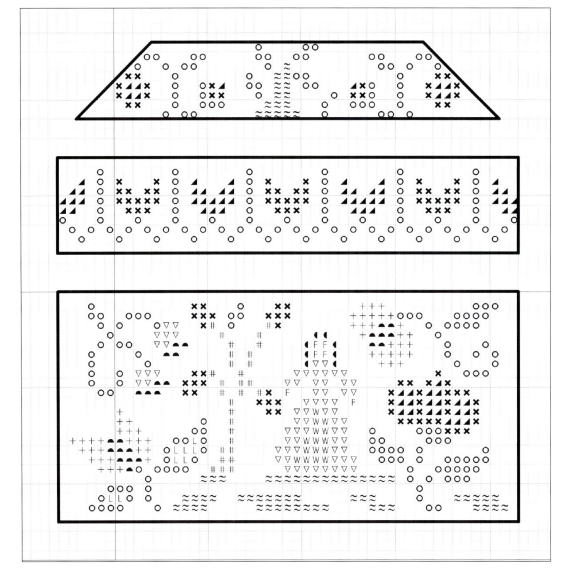

Casket-Left and Right Side

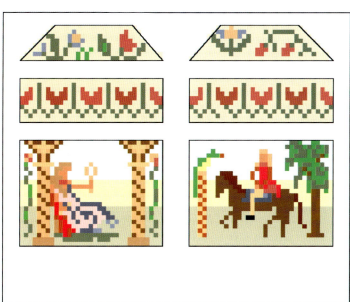

Photos by Kevin Hosley

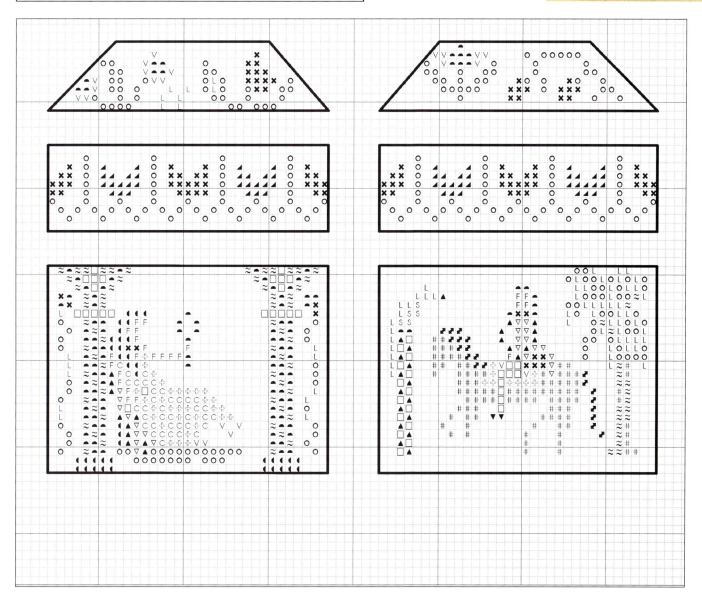

PROJECT #2.4
Mirror Surround
Designed by: Annelle Ferguson

Materials Needed:
    #60 silk gauze
    Silk sewing thread/embroidery floss

Stitch Count:
    75 (w) x 85 (h)
    Approx. finished size: 1¼ in. x 1⅜ in.

Color Chart:

Code	Color	Comparable to DMC #'s
✖	Dk. Green	3051
○	Med. Green	3052
B	Med. Brown	420
▼	Dk. Brown	433
●	Med. Blue	334
R	Tan	436
S	Lt. Blue	3325
I	Pale Blue	3756
❚	Dk. Rose	3350
+	Med. Rose	3731
Z	Lt. Rose	3354
◄	Bright Gold	782
▲	Black	413
V	White	
▽	Dk. Gold	3045
—	Med. Gold	729
L	Lt. Gold	677
□	Off-White (Background)	3033

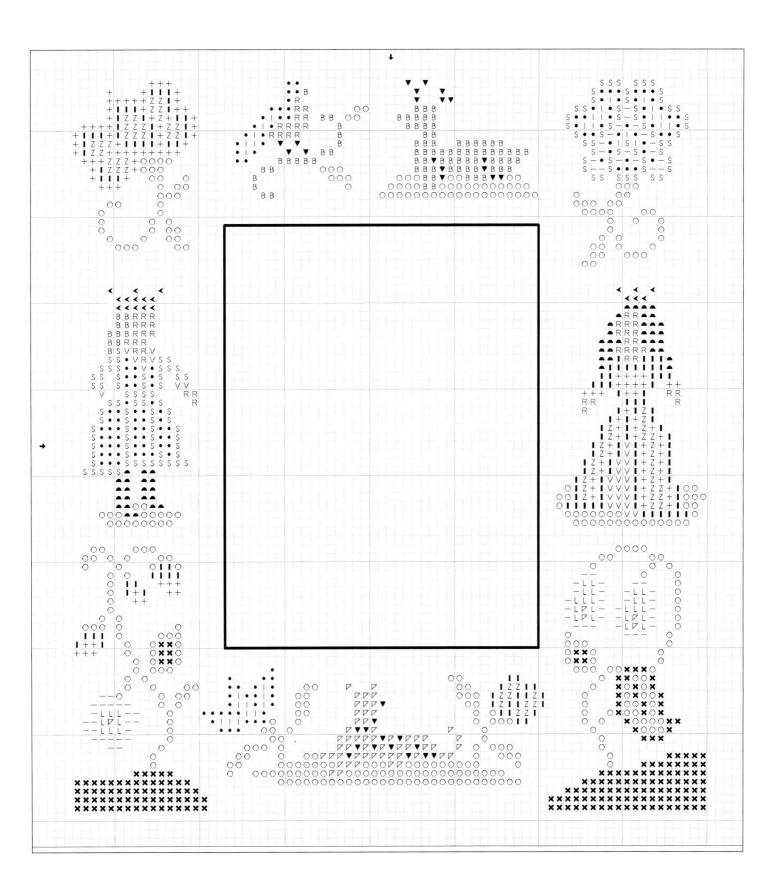

PROJECT #2.5
17th Century Floral Repeat Design
Designed by: Rosemary Conway-Jones

Materials Needed:
   #48 (or smaller) silk gauze
   DMC embroidery floss

Color Chart:

Code	Color	Comparable to DMC #'s
/	Lt. Pink	223
+	Vy Dk. Green	500
▼	Dk. Green	501
S	Med. Green	502
○	Med. Khaki Green	3012
●	Lt. Khaki Green	3013
▽	Gold	3046
×	Med. Peach	3779
		Lt. Turquoise	3811
□	Beige (Background)	842

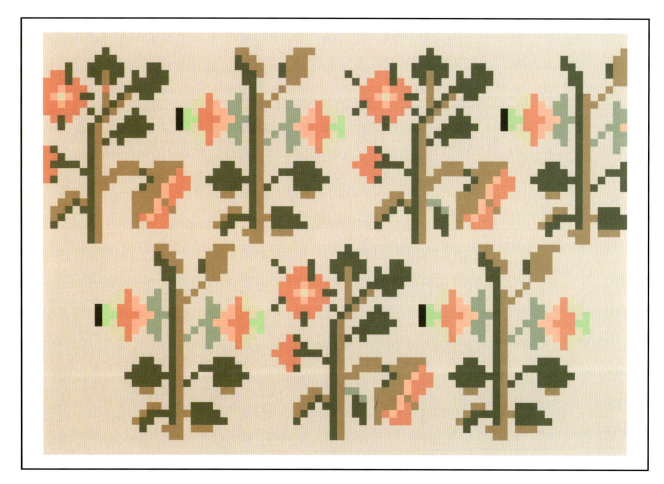

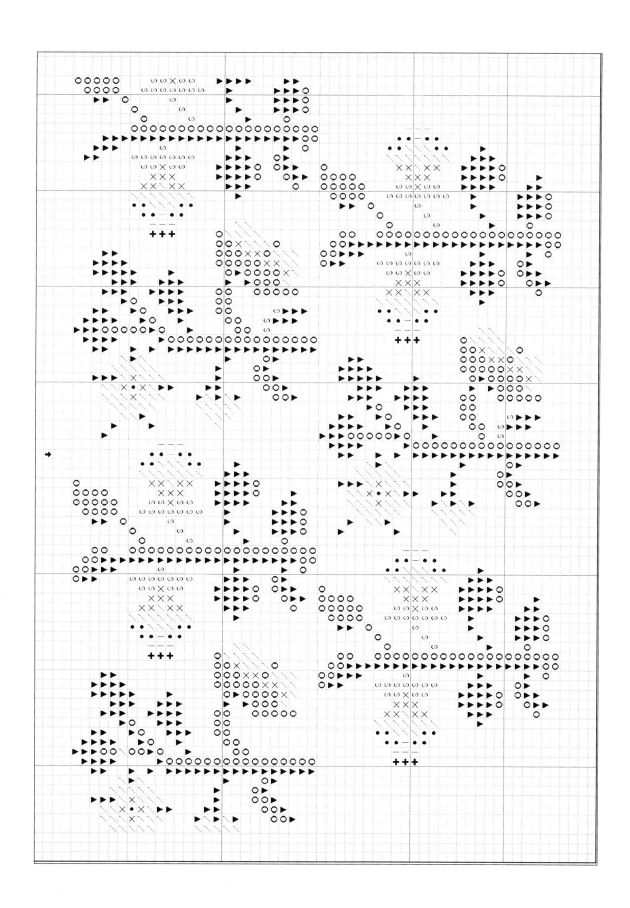

PROJECT #2.6
17th Century Florentine Pattern
Designed by: Martha Crowe

Materials Needed:
  #40 (or smaller) silk gauze
  DMC embroidery floss
  Approx. size of wing chair:
      4³/8 in. (h) x 3³/4 in. (w)

Color Chart:

Order of Colors	Comparable to DMC #'s
Dk. Rust	918
Med. Rust	920
Lt. Rust	921
Vy. Lt. Rust	922
Dk. Blue	796
Med. Blue	792
Green	733

Note: Use Bargello stitch (over 4 threads).

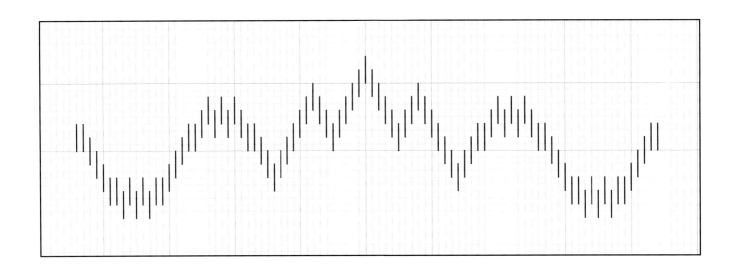

Chapter 3

18th-Century
English Needlework

Individuality of expression is the beginning and end of all art.
—Jahann Wofgang von Goethe (1749-1832)

The decades covering the reigns of Queen Anne (1702-1714) and George I (1714-1727) were times of stability for England. The middle class was becoming more affluent and was giving greater attention to the beauty of its homes and surroundings. Needlework continued to be an important and fashionable task for ladies of the upper and middle class, as well as for royalty. At Hampton Court, Queen Anne discovered many embroidered items, hangings and chair and stool coverings made by the late Queen Mary and her ladies of the court. Many of the techniques used on 17th-century embroidery were carried over into the new century. Used for more practical purposes, needlework centered on adult interests, not on the learning activities of children.

Queen Anne was the daughter of James II, the sister to Queen Mary, and the last of the Stuarts. During her short reign, a new style of decorative arts emerged that was to continue for many years into the Georgian period. In *Needlework Styles for Period Furniture*, Hope Hanley writes about the Queen Anne style of furniture: "Form and proportion best describes the Queen Anne period. To most people, Queen Anne is a classic, easily identifiable style. Later styles may be bolder or more elegant, but Queen Anne retains a purity of line and proportion that pleases the eye even today." The gentle curved lines of Queen Anne furniture offered a pleasing contrast to the characteristic straight lines of the William and Mary style.

Crewel embroidery continued to be used for bed hangings and costumes well into the 18th century. From the large baroque flowers and leaves, the patterns were transformed into smaller and more delicate designs of floral sprays and clusters. By 1750, crewelwork for bed hangings and coverlets had fallen from favor.

Particular attention was given to costumes, especially for formal wear. Ladies' dresses and men's waistcoats were lavishly decorated with crewelwork on silk and velvet materials. Professional designers were usually responsible for the ornately embroidered waistcoats. The luxurious fabrics could be purchased with the embroidery already stitched. A tailor would cut the design area to the customer's size and shape, add a plain backing, and complete the garment. For women, an entire gown could be embroidered. However, for more informal dress, the embroidery would be confined to the stomacher. Stomachers were triangular pieces of fabric made to fit into the V-shaped bodice of a gown. The designs

Doll with stomacher designed by Susan Sirkis. The stomacher is embroidered with silk and metallic thread in laid thread and chain stitching. Accents are worked in French knots and cross stitches. Approximate finished size: 3/4 in. wide at top, 1 1/2 in. high. Project 3.1. Figure by Joan Benzell.

were worked on bright colored silks with the floral motifs following the length of the triangle.

During the first half of the 18th century, embroiderers turned their energies to canvas work. Tent stitch on canvas fabric became the most favored technique used for furnishings. It was used for upholstery, wall hangings, fire screens, card table surfaces and carpets.

The reign of George II (1727-1760), and the beginning of the Georgian period, coincides with the activity of the famed cabinetmaker, Thomas Chippendale. Chippendale published his first catalog, *The Gentleman and Cabinet-Makers Director*, in 1754. His influence was followed by George Hepplewhite and Thomas Sheraton later in the century. Decorative needlework of superior quality and beauty was created by amateurs and professionals for furniture pieces by Queen Anne and Georgian craftsmen.

The popularity of using canvas work for upholstery peaked in 18th-century England. By early in the century, the upholsterer was influential in organizing and directing the complete

Photo by Mary and Tom Kaliski

Sue Bakker needlepoint upholstery on Patrick Puttock Gainsborough chair. George I bureau and Philadelphia dressing table by Patrick Puttock. Margaret Nine hand-colored original antique engraving. Porcelain French jardinière and floral bouquet by Le Chateau Interiors.

Photo by Mary and Tom Kaliski

Slipper chair made by Betty Valentine with needle-worked upholstery by Annelle Ferguson.

furnishing of a house. The most well-known upholsterer of the period was Thomas Chippendale. He was not only responsible for the making of furniture in his workshop, but had in his employ other craftsmen for specialized work.

A large number of canvas embroideries were used for covering the seats and backs of side chairs. Very often, the needleworked piece was designed especially for a particular chair or the needlework was made first, then an appropriate chair was constructed for it. The border designs would then follow the frame and shape of the chair seat and back. Winged chairs were also frequently decorated with canvas embroidery. Designs for both styles of seating displayed the love the English had for floral patterns, no doubt inspired by their love of gardens.

Subject matter for chair seat patterns varied. Large bouquets of naturalistic flowers, tied with ribbons or overflowing from a cornucopia, were popular designs. Single urns, vases or baskets were shown filled with blooms. Chinese birds,

Slipper chair and settee with Oriental scene by Betty Valentine; side chair by Carol Hardy, shepherdess with floral border on seat; all designed by Annelle Ferguson. Projects 3.2, 3.4, 3.7.

flowers and the stylized blue and white patterns of chinoiserie were favorite designs for containers. An all-over floral design showing the flowers extending outward from one stem was frequently used. Other choices, used often in the 1730s and 1740s, were pastoral or pictorial scenes surrounded by borders of flowers and foliage in bright colors. The centers were usually based on classical scenes taken from engraved sources. An exceptional example of this pattern style is found on a set of six chair and settee coverings in the Victoria and Albert Museum, London. Each piece is decorated with a different scene based on William Kent's illustrations for John Gay's *Fables*. Each scene has a bold and decorative floral border.

Winged chairs were often fully upholstered with elaborate canvas embroidery. The entire pattern would spread over the seat and back, and onto the wings of the chair. The designs ranged from pictorial scenes taken from the classics and the Bible, to floral arrangements. A catalog showing "The Twelve Months of

"The Poet and the Rose" full-size chair seat (t.477.1970), English c. 1730, Victoria and Albert Museum.

Needleworked chair seat of landscaped rural setting with floral border, English, c. 1750. Annelle Ferguson.

Flowers" was published about 1730 in London by Robert Furber. Large bouquets in elegant vases displayed the flowers for each month. Many needleworked chair patterns were inspired by these floral prints.

Small items such as pin cushions and various styles of bags were often worked on canvas. Hand-held screens, which were used to protect the face from the heat of the fireplace, were popular needleworked accessories. In large rooms, several might have been placed about, ready for use. Embroidered panels continued to be in vogue until the last quarter of the 18th century. They were decorated with floral designs similar to the patterns used for chair seats.

For more practical reasons, panels for pole screens were favorite canvas-worked items. Pole screens served the same purpose as hand screens, they could be highly decorative and they were useful objects to have in a room. Placed in a suitable position for protection from the fire, the screen did not receive the same wear and tear as chair seats; therefore, the beauty of the design remained for many years. In a June 1994 article by Geoffrey Beard in *The Magazine Antiques*, Mr. Beard states: "Excesses were not unknown. One exasperated husband complained in 1758 that 'we have twice as many fire screens as chimneys,' thanks to his wife, who kept their daughters incessantly at work with the needle."

Card playing had always been a favorite pastime among the wealthy in England. The Queen Anne period produced the first hinged, folding card tables. This was yet another vehicle for decorative needlework. Tent stitched pictures were popular throughout the 18th century. Somewhat larger than the panels created for pole screens, the card table panel's focal point may have been a country squire and his lady looking out over a rural area. The scene would include a brick house, other people at work, various animals at play and large birds flying over the landscape. Wall hangings were equally fashionable but have not survived well. The same design elements that were worked on card tables were carried out on tall, narrower, canvas-worked panels and then set into the plaster of the walls.

Needleworked carpets in the 18th century

Eighteenth-century English floral panel, designed by Annelle Ferguson, based on an original from Malletts, London. Framed by Margaret Nine. Chest by Roger Gutheil, vase by Le Chateau Interiors. Project 3.6.

Pole screen by Roger Gutheil, needleworked panel by Annelle Ferguson, flowers by Sandra Wall. Nelson Kline collection. (*Miniature Collector*, September/October, 1994, p. 39)

were intended to be used on the floor. These were sometimes made professionally, but more often, may have been the work of the amateur. A basic design was an array of large flowers and leaves in a profusion of colors covering the entire canvas. Other designs depicted bouquets of flowers rising from vases and baskets, with both styles having deep floral borders. Around 1760, geometric patterns replaced the floral border or the main central area.

Sampler making continued to be popular and part of a young girl's education during the 18th century. Most samplers were now made in schools as exercises for learning alphabets, numerals, moral sayings and Bible verses, as well as for learning sewing. The long narrow band of the 17th century changed into a more squared shape with a wide border. The new styles used patterns and motifs from earlier periods as selected by the individual teachers. When completed, the samplers were hung on the wall in the home for proud parents and relatives to view. The designs contained rows of alphabets, texts and familiar motifs such as birds, flowers, and the ever-popular coronet. The lower section was often filled with a landscaped scene, and all was set within a stylized border.

Annelle Ferguson floral design on polescreen by Roger Gutheil. Project 3.8.

Sue Bakker floral carpet, adapted from an 18th century (c. 1740) wool carpet. The original measures 8'4" x 5' 6" and is from the collection of Mallett & Son, London. The floral spray in the central panel, framed within a border of flowers, is pictured on p. 110 in *Antique Needlework* by Lanto Synge. Project 3.7.

Tree of Life chair seat by Judith Ohanian. Project 3.3.

Stitching map samplers developed towards the end of the century. The technique combined learning basic needlework with studying geography. Map samplers were usually worked in black thread, outlining local villages and small towns. Some were made into three-dimensional globe samplers showing countries and continents. Also in the schoolroom at the turn of the century, young children created darning samplers. Holes were cut into the fabric and then mended using a variety of darning stitches. This was considered necessary training for the future homemaker who would be responsible for repairing her household linens and clothes.

After 1770 there was a decline in canvas-worked embroidery. Due to the Industrial Revolution, England experienced numerous economic and social changes. However, the Queen Anne and Georgian decades are considered England's greatest period of decorative creativity.

Photo by Annelle Ferguson

Eighteenth century, English style sampler designed by Annelle Ferguson.

Chapter 3 *Projects*
18th-Century English Needlework

All projects are for personal use only. They may not be stitched and sold for profit.

PROJECT #3.1

Stomacher
Designed by: Susan Sirkis

Stomachers were worn in the 17th and 18th centuries. Pinned under the bodice opening, the stomacher concealed the stays (corset) and chemise. Often the stomacher was made of the same fabric as the dress. Sometimes the stomacher was elaborately embroidered with a variety of stitches—the same stitches used to embellish other articles of wearing apparel and household items. Satin, stem and buttonhole were used—still familiar to us today. Chain stitching was accomplished in the same way we do today, needleworked on the surface of the fabric. It was also accomplished with the use of a tiny hook fixed into a handle. These tools were called *tambour hooks*; the work to which they referred was called *tambour*. The name was derived from the circular frames necessary to the completion of the work, in other words, embroidery hoops.

Motifs used on the stomachers included many of the same naturalistic designs used in crewel embroidery. Worked on silk backgrounds with very fine silk threads, the appearance of the designs was entirely different from the larger designs worked in woolen threads.

Material and Tools

Lightweight, washable silk, white or eggshell
Embroidery hoop
Pencil
Sulky (rayon thread for machine embroidery)
   or silk sewing thread (green, yellow, pink)
#20 between needle
Metallic gold thread
Padded pinning board
Iron
Medium-weight buckram or index card
Woolite®

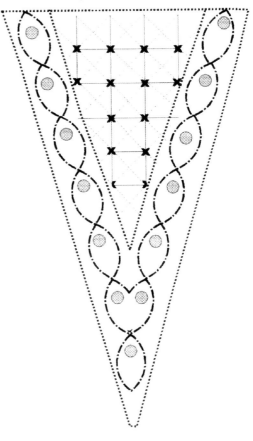

Enlarged to show detail

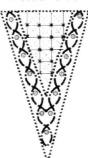

Actual Size

Full-size
stomacher pattern

Stretch silk on an embroidery hoop. Trace the design in light pencil strokes. Using Sulky or silk sewing thread and a #20 between needle, work the design as indicated. To make the laid stitches, put down the single-thread long stitches of the green first. Next, lay down the diagonal metallic gold stitches. Work the pink cross stitches at the interstices.

When the embroidery is complete, remove it from the hoop and wash gently in Woolite®. Lay upside down on a padded pinning board and stretch into shape. Allow to dry. Press the wrong side with a warm iron if needed. Trace the stomacher pattern piece on buckram or index card. When you have cut the stomacher out, lay the embroidery over it and trim away excess, leaving only a 1/4 inch seam allowance. Turn the seam allowance over the edges of the buckram, mitering each corner. Baste in place. Cut another piece of plain silk the same size and baste under the seam allowance. Whip to the back of the stomacher. If the stomacher is to be glued in place to the front of the doll, the lining may be omitted.

Single strand of thread

....	Chain stitch - Soft Yellow
————————	Laid thread - Green
— · — · — · — · —	Chain stitch - Green
· · · · · · · · · · ·	Laid thread - Metallic Gold
✗	Cross stitch
＇	Half cross stitch
◎	French knot - Pink (three times around the needle)

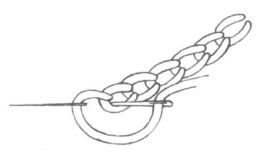

Chain stitches are a series of loop stitches. Take care that the loop sizes remain consistent.

PROJECT #3.2
Slipper Chair Back and Seat Cover
Designed by: Annelle Ferguson

Photos by Mary Kaliski

Materials Needed:
> #48 silk gauze
> DMC embroidery floss

Stitch Count:
> 57 (w) x 87 (h) Back Cover
> 63 (w) x 57 (h) Seat Cover
> Approx. size of chair:
>> 3³/₄ in. (h) x 1¹/₂ in. (w)

Color Chart:

Code	Color	Comparable to DMC #'s
•	Dk. Rust	355
▽	Med. Rust	356
×	Off-White	746
—	Blue	926
S	Med. Blue	3768
+	Dk. Blue	924
○	Med. Green	3053
I	Dk. Green	3051
	Dk. Blue (Inside Panel Background)	924
	Dk. Rust (Outside Border Background)	355

PROJECT #3.3
Tree of Life
Designed by: Judith Ohanian

Materials Needed:
- #40 OR #48 silk gauze
- DMC embroidery floss

Stitch Count:
77 (w) x 59 (h)

Approx. size of chair:
3 in. (h) x 1¾ in. (w)

Color Chart:

Code	Color	Comparable to DMC #'s
N	Lt. Peach	758
●	Med. Peach	3064
⋈	Dk. Terra Cotta	355
L	Lt. Avocado Green	470
·	Med. Grey Green	3052
I	Dk. Avocado Green	936
▼	Dk. Coffee Brown	801
✕	Dk. Beige Brown	839
○	Black Brown	3371
○	Lt. Mauve	778
+	Med. Mauve	316
◣	Dk. Mauve	315
C	Med. Gold	729
8	Topaz	725
≡	Dk. Topaz	781
△	Lt. Baby Blue	3325
B	Med. Baby Blue	334
—	Lt. Navy	322
↙	Med. Navy	311
□	Off White (Background)	712

Backstitches are always worked after the needlepoint has been done. The stitches can travel in any direction and can be worked over more than one needlepoint stitch. Pull the stitches only tight enough for them to lay flat. Work backstitches in the following colors: Leaves - 3052 Med. Grey Green, Red flower - 355 Dk. Terra Cotta

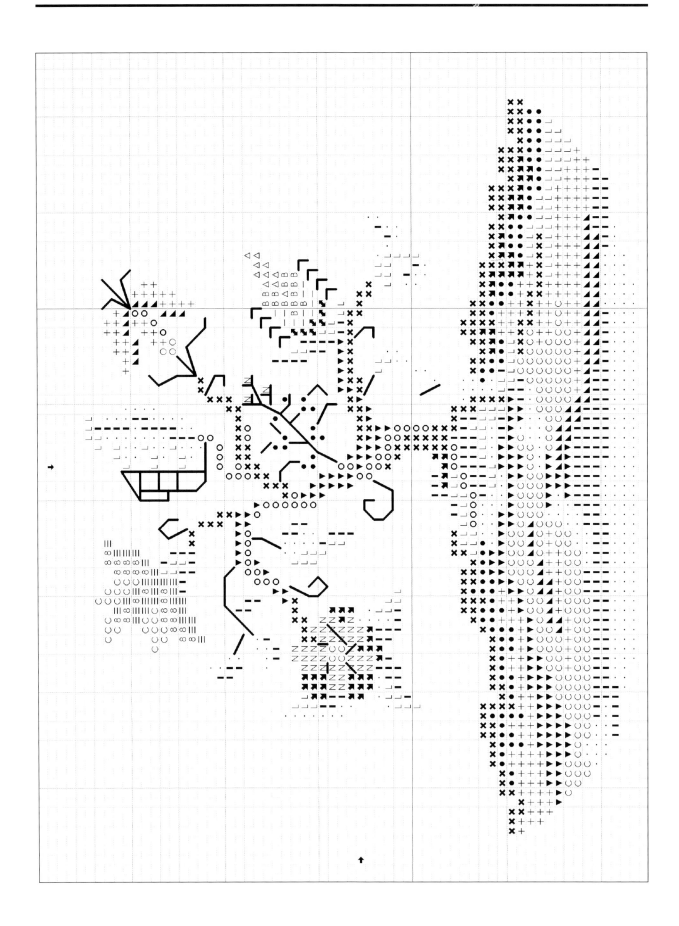

PROJECT #3.4
Oriental Design for Bench Seat

Designed by: Annelle Ferguson

Photo by Mary Kaliski

Materials Needed:
    #48 silk gauze
    DMC embroidery floss

Stitch Count:
    189 (w) x 63 (h)

Color Chart:

Code	Color	Comparable to DMC #'s
○	Dk. Rust	355
╱	Med. Rust	356
L	Lt. Tan	543
✖	Dk. Blue	924
▽	Brown	434
➤	Dk. Green	3051
+	Med. Green	3052
Z	Lt. Green	3053
I	Med. Brown	436
S	Med. Blue	3768
□	Off-White (Background)	3033

Circled code indicates filling in background with that color.

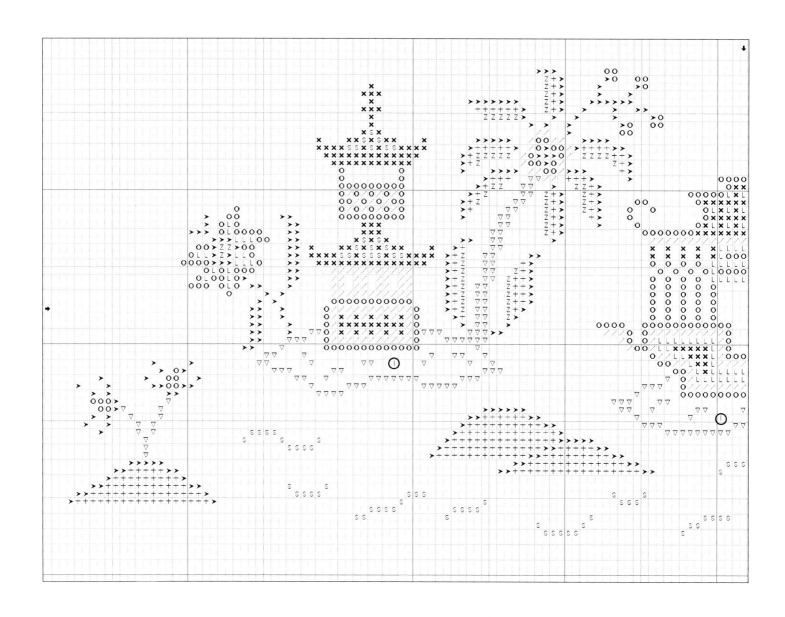

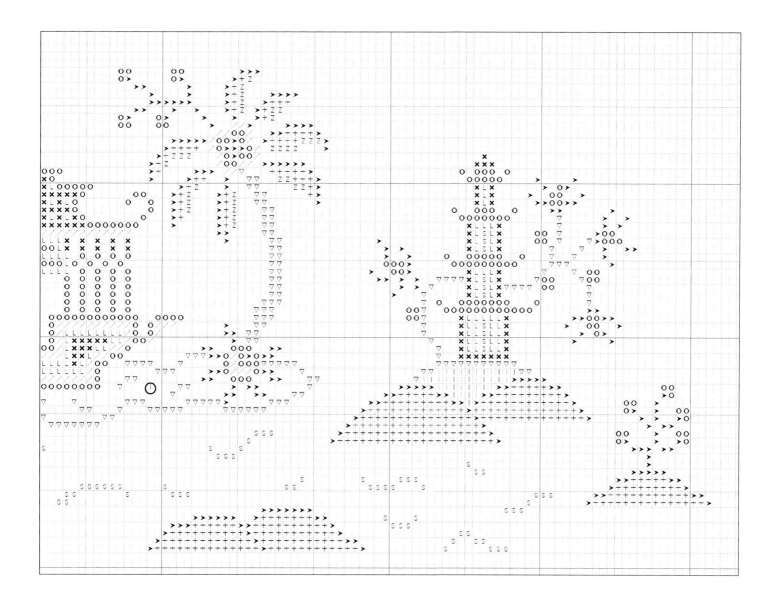

PROJECT #3.5

Shepherdess with Floral Border Chair Seat

Designed by: Annelle Ferguson

Materials Needed:

Silk sewing thread/embroidery floss

Stitch Count :

95 (w) x 71 (h)

Approx. size of chair:

3 1/2 in. (h) x 1 3/4 in. (w)

Approx. size of seat:

1 3/4 in. x 1 1/2 in.

Photo by Mary Kaliski

Color Chart

Code	Color	Comparable to DMC #'s
∕	Lt. Blue	3753
Z	Med. Blue	932
•	Dk. Blue (Border Background)	930
△	Brown	433
▐	Dk. Brown	869
✚	Dk. Green	3051
⊠	Med. Green	3052
✕	Lt. Green	3053
◤	Black	844
○	Lt. Peach	3713
S	Med. Peach	3712
▼	Dk. Peach	347
−	Flesh	3773
⊳	Lt. Gold	746
U	Med. Gold	677
◖	Dk. Gold	729
□	Ecru (Landscape Background)	

Circled code indicates filling in background with that color

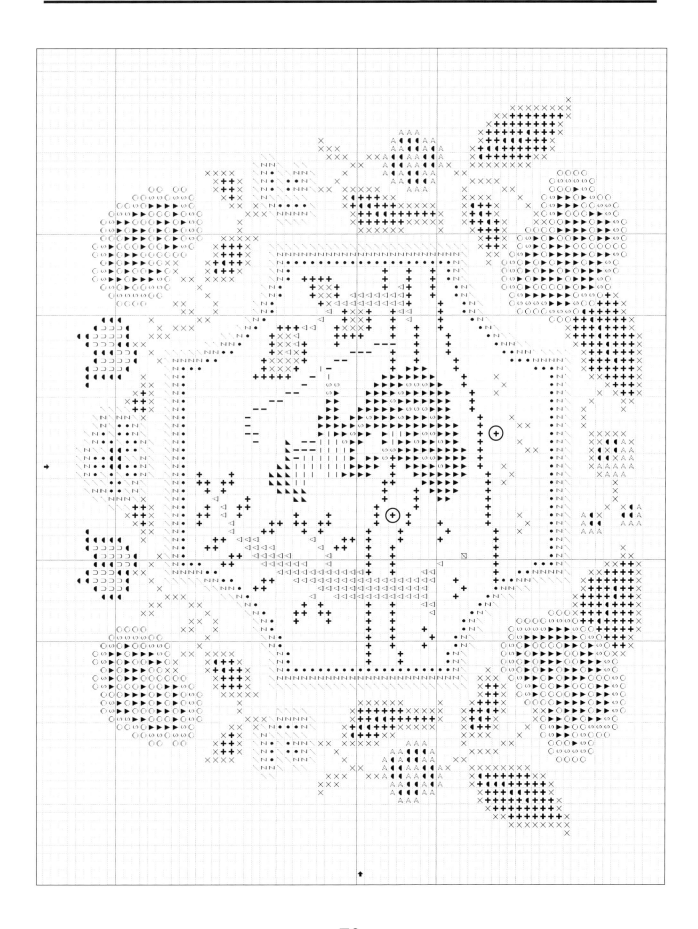

PROJECT #3.6
Floral Arrangement
Designed by: Annelle Ferguson

Materials Needed:
> #60 or smaller silk gauze
> Silk sewing thread/embroidery floss

Stitch Count:
> 87 (w) x 111 (h)

Color Chart:

Code	Color	Comparable to DMC #'s
I	Lt. Peach	951
S	Med. Peach	356
•	Dk. Peach	355
×	Lt. Gray/Green	3053
Z	Med. Gray/Green	3052
➤	Dk. Gray/Green	3051
▽	Med. Golden Tan	3045
—	Off-White	822
E	Ecru	
○	Lt. Pine Green	772
+	Med. Pine Green	3363
B	Med. Blue	926
L	Lt. Blue	928
V	Med. Gold	676
∕	Lt. Gold	746

PROJECT #3.7A & B
English Garden
Designed by: Sue Bakker

Materials Needed:
> #40 silk gauze
> DMC embroidery floss

Stitch Count:
> 341(w) x 225 (h)
> Finished size: 4$\frac{1}{8}$ in. x 7$\frac{3}{8}$ in.

Color Chart:

Code	Color	Comparable to DMC #'s
▼	Dk. Hazel Nut Brown	420
▽	Lt. Hazel Nut Brown	422
✚	Dk. Gold	3828
E	Med. Gold	729
▽	Lt. Gold	676
/	Pale Gold	3047
▶	Lt. Brown	435
●	Dk. Green	3011
—	Med. Green	3012
I	Lt. Green	3013
✖	Dk. Salmon	3328
○	Off White	543
▮	Vy. Dk. Grey Green	924

Code	Color	Comparable to DMC #'s
➤	Dk. Grey Green	3768
+	Med. Grey Green	926
L	Lt. Grey Green	927
S	Vy. Lt. Grey Green	928
U	Lt. Beaver Grey	3072
✕	Med. Blue	931
Z	Med. Mauve	3041
▲	Dk. Brown	3021
o	Dk. Grey	535
·	Med. Grey	648
	Lt. Brown (Background for Border)	840
	Lt. Grey Green (Background for Center)	927

PROJECT #3.8
Floral Panel for Firescreen
Designed by: Annelle Ferguson

Materials Needed:
>   #60 silk gauze
>   Silk sewing thread/embroidery floss

Stitch Count:
>   73 (w) x 73 (h)
>   Polescreen approx. 4 1/4 in. (h)
>   Approx. size of panel: 1 1/4 in. x 1 1/4 in.

Color Chart:

Code	Color	Comparable to DMC #'s
Z	Dk. Tangerine	722
—	Yellow	745
▽	Lt. Gold	746
•	Med. Gold	677
ı	Dk. Gold	729
o	Dk. Salmon	347
S	Med. Salmon	3328
+	Lt. Salmon	760
▽	Dk. Green	469
×	Med. Green	470
/	Lt. Green	472
➤	Med. Blue	931
V	Blue	3752
L	Lt. Blue	3753
□	Black (Border Background)	3799
	Ecru (Inside Arch Background)	

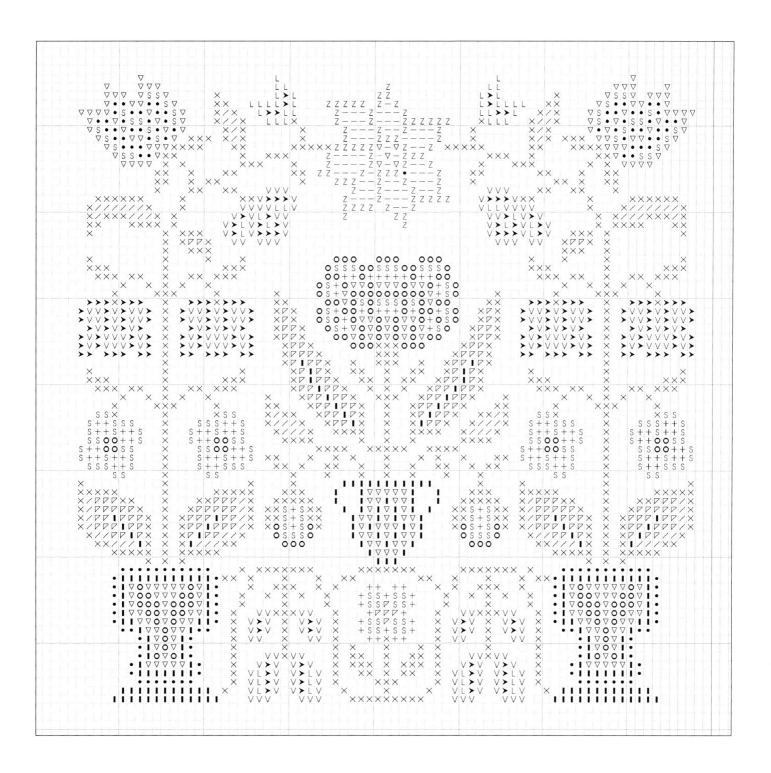

Chapter 4

18th-Century
American Needlework

Few things are impossible to diligence and skill.
—Samuel Johnson (1709-1784)

Throughout the 17th century, English colonization in the New World flourished. Before setting out across the Atlantic Ocean, the early settlers were often told to take with them enough household articles to last for some time. It seems likely that the women would have taken their sewing supplies aboard ship. Women would have needed to keep what clothing and linens the family owned mended at all times. Although most of the colonists were from the middle and lower classes, no woman, regardless of her social status, grew up without learning how to do basic needlework.

It was not until the beginning of the 18th century that the colonial population had grown large enough to begin establishing its own traditions. Until then, they were a people building a

Crewelwork bed covering by Jean Strup. Sampler designed by Annelle Ferguson and stitched by Esther Robertson. *Twin Manors* bedroom, The Toy and Miniatures Museum of Kansas City collection.

Photo courtesy of Toy and Miniature Museum of Kansas City

country out of the wilderness and the women usually worked with the men in creating a new life for themselves. However, in spite of all the hardships, women continued to sew and they taught their daughters to sew.

American needlework was at its finest in the 18th century. It was often considered a valuable household possession and is found listed in wills and inventories. All women learned plain sewing and marking as children. Decorative needlework was usually reserved for the privileged, a luxury for those women who could afford the materials.

As living conditions became more comfortable, a need arose for finer furnishings. The New England communities were well established by mid-century and women had more leisure time to spend on fancy needlework. Decorative embroideries, being a woman's most important accomplishment, became cherished keepsakes and were handed down from generation to generation. The largest number of crewel embroideries from the 18th century are bedcoverings. The bed was an important piece of furniture and was usually placed in the parlor of a colonial home. Crewelwork decorating the bedcoverings and hangings was one indication of wealth and a source of pride for the embroiderer.

Designs on bedcoverings were similar to the floral patterns of English origin. Due to a need to economize on thread, the motifs were more open and spacious and not as bold and detailed as their English counterparts. Also, if the stitcher had prepared her own linen, she was quite proud of the finished product and hesitated to hide it under stitches of woolen yarn. These concerns contributed to a unique and exclusive American design style that was popular until midcentury.

Crewel designs were often found on clothing for the colonial family. Floral motifs were worked on slippers, gowns for women and children, men's waistcoats, petticoat borders and pockets. Embroidered borders on petticoats with motifs of trees, flowers and animal scenes following one another, were colorful and enchanting. The borders could be removed from a worn-out skirt and reattached to a new skirt. Quite charming were the single pockets worn by women in midcentury. The pear-shaped bags were tied around the waist and worn over the petticoat. Slits in the gown enabled ladies to reach into their pockets that held such articles as keys, coins, sewing implements and personal treasures. Working women often wore their pocket on the outside of the dress, but underneath their aprons. Floral designs were most common with each motif connecting to another by flowing vines.

Linen was the most commonly used background fabric. It was usually imported and was available in the town shops or from a peddler's wagon. Materials could also be bought from instructors who taught embroidery. Often, the linen used was manufactured in the home. Several New England colonies encouraged households to plant and raise flax or hemp. In many colonial homes, daily chores included spinning and weaving, producing linen and woolen cloth. The imported crewels were as expensive as the linen fabric. Many homemakers dyed their own thread, being taught by Indian women how to use native plants and trees to produce a variety of colors. Some dyes were made from onions for yellows, elderberries for lavender, and walnut bark for browns. The indigo plant was an American product and was used for shades of blue. Some early New England crewelwork is embroidered entirely in indigo-dyed wools on white linen.

Photo courtesy of Esther Robertson

Sampler designed by Annelle Ferguson and stitched by Esther Robertson. The design is in the style of 18th-century samplers from the Newbury, Massachusetts, area. Popular motifs such as the running deer were found on many canvas worked pieces referred to as the "Fishing Lady" series. The Toy and Miniature Museum of Kansas City collection.

By the middle of the 17th century, most large New England towns had established dame schools for younger children, both boys and girls. However, after dame school, boys went on to study Latin and mathematics and girls remained in the home, being taught by their mothers. At the beginning of the 18th century, many families desired to further the education of their daughters. In 1706, Mary Turfrey, from Boston, was the first to advertise a finishing school for girls. Sampler making soon became a major part of a properly reared young girl's education. In *The Book of Samplers*, Marguerite Fawdry and Deborah Brown write, "If the 17th century is rightly regarded as the golden age of the sampler in England, the 18th century certainly saw the coming of age of the American sampler." Samplers spanned the whole of the early American period. Most surviving samplers were made between 1785 and 1840 and are products of schoolgirl instruction.

The 18th-century woman did not limit her embroidery to crewelworked bedcoverings, hangings, and clothing. Canvas work was just as popular in the colonies as in England. The most attractive and picturesque early American work was produced between the years 1700 and 1780. Most properly taught colonial housewives devoted many hours creating decorative textiles for the home, items that were useful as well as beautiful. Fancy needlework was a woman's most important contribution to her household. All of her achievements were greatly appreciated by family members and also admired by all who saw them.

Professional embroiderers worked in New England and many offered instruction in the technique of using *tent*, *Florentine* and *cross* stitch for canvas work. Patterns were available from England and from professional patternmakers in the colonies. Canvases purchased with designs already drawn on them were imported, but lessons were offered to those who wished to create their own patterns. Mrs. Susannah Condy operated a school in Boston but also offered for sale materials for canvas work. In *The Needleworker's Dictionary*, Pamela Clabburn quotes from an ad in a 1738 Boston newspaper, "To be had at Mrs. Condy's near the Old North Meeting House; all sorts of beautiful figures on Canvas for Tent Stitch; the patterns from London, but drawn by her much cheaper than English drawing; All sorts of Canvas without drawing..."

Room setting designed and built by Peter Kendall. Dressing table and chair by Gerald Crawford. Mirror made by John Hodgson, embellished by Le Chateau Ineriors (Frank Hanley & Jeffery Guéno). Needleworked chair seat by Annelle Ferguson. Project 4.2.

Photo by Anne Day Smith

Canvas work was used for a variety of reasons in colonial America. Onto a fine canvas fabric that had between 22 and 52 holes per inch, the tent stitch was applied to both design and background area using crewel yarns. This technique was often used for seat covers, firescreen panels, game table tops, pocket books, bed rugs and pictorial needlework. Color selection was always the choice of the stitcher, who had learned shading as part of her needlework education.

Early American craftsmen often referred to the furniture catalogs from England, but soon devised their own distinct variations of the Queen Anne and Chippendale styles. The different characteristics were easily identified by the region or the name of the individual cabinetmaker. New England cabinetmakers produced more chairs

Betty Valentine chair with floral needleworked seat cover, game table with needleworked panel in recessed top, and settee with needleworked seat cushion. All needlework designed by Annelle Ferguson. Hand-held fire screen by Judith Ohanian. Projects 4.4, 4.5, 4.6, 4.7.

than any other type of furniture. Needlework was very often applied to the style of side chair that was currently in fashion. Most chair seat upholstery was worked by an experienced stitcher. Floral designs, very similar to the English florals but more spacious, were frequently created to fit a specific chair. Popular in the colonies, as in England, were pictorial subjects surrounded by floral borders.

American needleworkers produced numerous Florentine stitch designs, using the flame pattern or a stylized geometric pattern. A covering on a 1720 Queen Anne wing chair in the collection of the Metropolitan Museum of Art, New York City, is an exceptional example of a Florentine repeat pattern. The front of the chair is upholstered in a repeating carnation pattern with alternating colors. Due to the size of the chair, the upholstery may have been worked in a professional workshop. The needlework covering the back is an enchanting landscape with birds in flight, running deer, a shepherd tending his flock of sheep and ducks floating on a pond. This panel was probably worked by an

Winged chair designed and upholstered by Charles Krug, shown in parlor of *Peyton-Randolph House*, designed and built by Peter Kendall. Repeat design by Annelle Ferguson. Sewing table by James Hastrich, painting on door wall by Paul Saltarelli.

amateur, perhaps by the wife of the original owner. Repeating patterns remained popular for chair-seat upholstery until midcentury.

The same floral styles created for chair-seat covers were often found on fire-screen panels which were useful in winter when staying warm meant sitting close to the fire.

Although frowned upon in 17th-century New England, card playing was a fashionable form of entertainment in the 18th century. The activity was enjoyed in private homes and in public inns and taverns. Inventories indicate that card tables were found in several locations in the home, their style usually complementing the other furniture in the room. Second only to chairs, gaming tables were the most frequently produced articles of furniture by New England cabinetmakers. The earliest examples were made in the Boston area as early as 1730. The Queen Anne styles had shallow recessed surfaces, originally intended for baize fabric, rounded or squared corners for candlesticks and scooped pockets for coins or counters. A drawer in front held cards and candles. Many were decorated with a needleworked panel, tacked into the

Full-size mahogany, white pine and maple game table with original needleworked top, Massachusetts, 1760-80. Measures 35¹³/₁₆ inches wide, 34³/₈ inches deep and 28³/₁₆ inches high. From The Chipstone Foundation, Milwaukee, Wisconsin.

recessed space. The hinged top was often closed to protect the needlework and the table was placed against a wall when not in use. The tables were typically light-weight, easy to lift and could be carried to a desired area and opened for game playing.

There are several superb examples in American museums. The Chipstone Foundation in Milwaukee, Wisconsin, has a Queen Anne game table with an embroidered top (Massachusetts, 1760-1780) displaying a floral arrangement stemming from a stylized vase surrounded by playing cards, coins and Chinese fish counters. Later, game tables from the Federal period had flat surfaces. With the top left half open, it presented an attractive setting when placed against a wall. Seldom mentioned in 18th-century furniture advertisements were embroidery stands. They were commonly used to prevent canvas distortion. Cabinetmakers

Lolling chair by Betty Valentine, upholstered by Donna Johnson. Chippendale chair by Tom Goad made in a Linda LaRoche class at the International Guild of Miniature Artisians' School; Queen Anne footstool by Betty Valentine; small footstool by Roger Gutheil. All needlework by Annelle Ferguson, based on 18th-century repeat patterns. Projects 4.8A, 4.8B, 4.8C, 4.8D.

Bed rug designed by Clarice Elder, bed by Wayne Crosby. Embroidery stand by Carol Hardy, needlework by Annelle Ferguson. Projects 4.9, 4.10.

were probably privately commissioned for such items. The surviving 18th-century floor frames were usually made of mahogany, a good hard wood that would not have warped from the tension caused by stretching the canvas. Toward the end of the century, cabinetmakers began producing sewing tables especially for holding all the sewing implements of the avid embroiderer. This small table was usually placed within reach of the embroidery frame, and by a favorite chair in which the embroiderer sat to do her fancy needlework.

The 18th-century embroiderer enjoyed creating small useful items that were currently in vogue. Geometric or floral motifs done in the Florentine stitch were frequently used on such functional articles as needlecases, pincushions, potholders and pocketbooks.

Pocketbooks were essentially used by men to carry their important papers and were popular from about 1740 to 1790. Most were constructed envelope style with a flap that folded over the opening or in a tri-fold design with pockets on each section. A colorful fabric was used for the lining, an attractive ribbon or trim was used around the edges.

In the early 18th century, the term *rugg* meant a cover for a bed. A bed rug, popular in the northern regions of New England, became known as a heavy woolen coverlet embroidered in woolen yarns. Large, bold, embroidered designs covered the majority of the surface, providing warmth and adding a decorative touch. Bed rugs were considered family treasures and have been handed down from generation to generation. They were surely a source of family pride as many surviving bed rugs have initials and dates included in the design.

Between 1725 and 1775, a collection of fascinating canvas-worked pictures, known as chimney pieces or fishing lady pictures, were made in the Boston area. It is believed these were worked by young women in their teens, perhaps as graduation pieces from a Boston finishing school. In 1923, Helen Bowen was the first to recognize the similarities among eight pictures and wrote of her findings in an *Antiques Magazine* article. By 1941, Nancy Graves Cabot had extended the research and wrote about 58 examples. Later, the total rose to 65 related embroideries.

The sizes vary from small ten-by-twelve-inch panels to large three-by-five-foot picturesque settings, but all share common elements. The entire canvas is filled with scenes of human figures, birds and animals, and flowers and trees, against a pastoral landscape. The main feature is usually a nicely dressed lady shown fishing in a pond. The larger pieces may have as many as three couples in the scene, while the smaller ones have only one couple. Other smaller panels often show a reclining shepherdess. It is probable that the canvases were drawn by Mrs. Susannah Condy, who advertised in Boston newspapers that her patterns were available to anyone who

Embroidered "Fishing Lady" picture, example of c.1750 Massachusetts embroidery, needleworked by Lynda Bauer. Original by Eunice Borune is in the Museum of Fine Arts, Boston. Design is from Cantitoe Corners, New York.

wanted them. Many of these exceptional embroidered pictures are found in museums and private collections. Sarah Warren was 18 years old in 1748 when she signed and dated her large chimney piece, which is now in the Winterthur Museum in Delaware. The Museum of Fine Arts, Boston, owns a smaller panel that is tacked onto a gaming table.

Needlework produced by American women in the 18th century is equal to the masterly accomplishments of other handcrafters of the period, such as woodworkers and silversmiths. A woman's ability to embroider was not only a means of self-expression but was also of economic value to her family. Daily chores usually included making and repairing clothing, making bed and table linens and creating decorative textiles for the home. The more affluent housewife could afford to spend more of her leisure time with her needle, eagerly contributing to the elegant furnishings of her home. However, techniques in design and application were to undergo drastic changes by the end of the 18th century. The artistic but time-consuming crewel- and canvas-worked designs faded from popularity due to a new fad, Berlin woolwork (Chapter 6), that changed needlework forever.

Game table by Paul Moore, needleworked panel designed by Duffy Wineman. Chairs by Roger Gutheil, bargello design by Martha Crowe. Candlestick by Emily Good, floorcloth by Ann Miller.

18th-Century American Needlework

All projects are for personal use only. They may not be stitched and sold for profit.

PROJECT #4.1
Crewel Bed Covering
Designed by: Cookie Ziemba

Materials Needed:
> Tracing paper
> Pencil
> Hot iron transfer pencil
> Paper towel
> Cotton balls
> Iron, ironing board
> Rust-proof glass headed pins and rust-proof regular pins
> Fine wool challis fabric, or other tightly woven
>   natural material
> #10 crewel needles
> DMC threads
> Embroidery hoop
> Embroidery scissors
> Magnification, if necessary

Photo by Mary and Tom Kaliski

General Directions:
- This was designed for a bed measuring 6¹/₂ in. long by 4³/4 in. wide.
- Use color photo of bedspread for color reference.
- It is best to use a plunging motion when embroidering, not the usual sewing motion.
- A hand-held embroidery hoop is essential as the bedspread will never lie flat enough if worked loosely in the hand.
- Use one strand of the DMC thread unless otherwise noted.

Method of Working:
1. Make a paper pattern of size needed out of paper towel, cut to shape, pin in place, draping and shaping it to see exact size needed for your bed.
2. Using your paper pattern, make an outline of the size of the bedspread with pencil, leaving enough extra fabric to fold under the pillow area. Plan where the motifs should be placed and mark these areas with pins so you can visualize placement.
3. Using tracing paper, make a copy of the actual size motifs, turn over tracing paper and recopy motifs on the back with hot iron transfer pencil. This will make your design face the same way as shown in the book.
4. Use the same procedure for the pillow top and three side panels.
5. Lay fabric out on ironing board and hold in place with glass-headed straight pins.
6. Allowing enough space for pillow motif and fold-over space, place traced center motif face down onto fabric. Pin in place with glass-headed straight pins.

7. Use dry iron at a medium high setting, and press *down* in one movement. *Do not go back and forth* in the usual ironing motion as it may smear design.

8. You may start embroidering any individual motif, complete all of them, and then "tie" it all together by doing the stems and branches last.

Finishing Bedspread:

9. If bedspread will be used for a four-poster bed, slit dropped part to accommodate bedposts.

10. Hem bedspread edges by folding back approximately ⅛ in. all around. Iron Stitch Witchery to hem.

11. Arrange on bed over pillows (cotton balls) and pin in place, including the top part that is folded over with pillows beneath. Wrap fabric completely around cotton balls, so they don't show at all.

Stitching Key:

A	Split Stitch
B	Feather Stitch
C	Outline Stitch (Stem)
D	Lazy Dazy
E	Satin Stitch
F	French Knots
G	Buttonhole Stitch
H	Filling Stitch

Color		Comparable to DMC #'s
Red	Light	225
	Medium	223
	Dark	221
Blue	Light	828
	Medium	932
	Dark	931
	Darkest	930
Green	Medium	3348
	Dark	3346
Gold		680
Brown		898

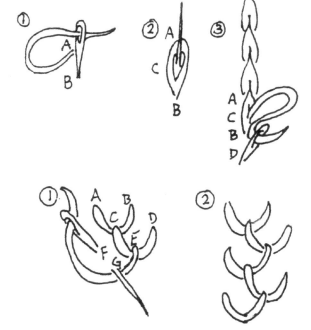

A   SPLIT STITCH

1. Go from A to B with a straight stitch. 2. Split through A-B, coming up through fabric and thread at center of C. 3. Work in continuous line.

B   FEATHER STITCH

1. Come at A and go down at B, come up at C and go down at D, making sure to leave a space in between, being sure to loop thread under needle.

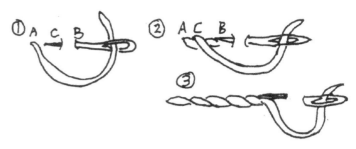

C   OUTLINE STITCH (STEM)
1. Come up at A, down at B, up at C, keeping
thread below needle. 2. Down at D, up at B,
coming up at the same hole. 3. Continue, always
keeping thread below needle. For broad areas such
as heavy branches, two threads may be used to
increase bulk.

D   LAZY DAZY
1. Come up through A and go down into same hole, forming loop. Come up at B
and down into C to secure the loop. In large Lazy Dazies, you may insert two
or three smaller loops, shading colors.

E   SATIN STITCH
Begin in center of motif, coming up at one edge, going down on other side.
Work across to first end of motif, slide needle under worked part and
start working again at the middle and moving outwards. This will help
in keeping stitches neat and properly angled.

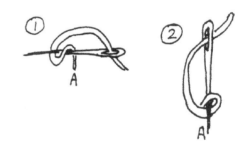

F   FRENCH KNOTS
1. Come up at A, twist thread once around needle.
2. Go through same hole, pull thread tightly, holding down
with nail, and push needle through fabric. You may need to
hold in place with thumb and forefinger as you push.
This is one of the few stitches that should be started with a
knot on the wrong side of fabric, as there is no room to start
with two back stitches.

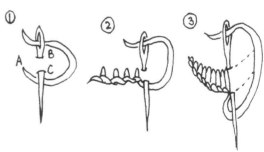

G   BUTTONHOLE STITCH
1. Come up at A, down at B, up at C, looping thread under
needle. 2. Continue along outer edge, keep needle vertical.
If filling an area, do not crowd together, allow a bit of
fabric to show through. If working with an arched area,
keep top of stitches quite close and fan out bottom of stitches.

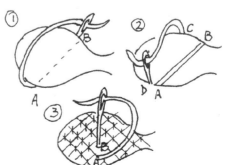

H   FILLING STITCH
1 & 2. Starting in center of motif, lay long stitches side by side,
A to B, coming up same side you go down, C to D. Leave a small
space between each stitch, complete filling in one direction.
Crisscross stitches using same color as 1 & 2, making a
diamond pattern. 3. Using a contrasting shade, tack down
each diamond, coming up at A and down in B.

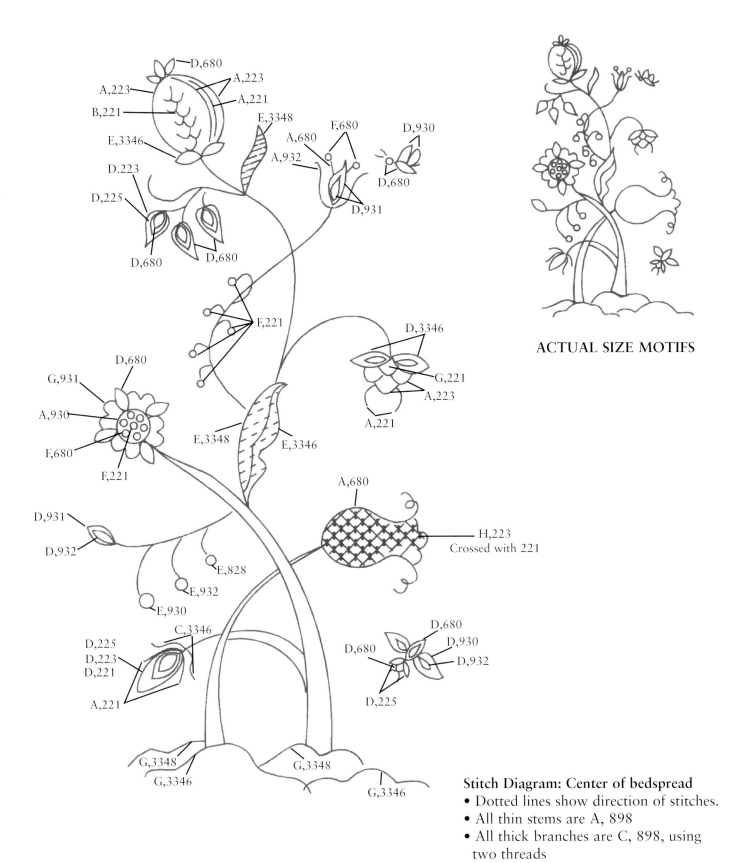

D,680
A,223
A,223
A,221
B,221
E,3348
F,680
A,680
D,930
E,3346
A,932
D,223
D,680
D,225
D,931
D,680
D,680
F,221
D,3346
D,680
G,931
G,221
A,930
A,223
F,680
F,221
A,221
E,3348
E,3346
A,680
D,931
D,932
H,223
Crossed with 221
E,828
E,932
E,930
C,3346
D,680
D,225
D,930
D,223
D,680
D,221
D,932
A,221
D,225
G,3348
G,3348
G,3346
G,3346

ACTUAL SIZE MOTIFS

Stitch Diagram: Center of bedspread
- Dotted lines show direction of stitches.
- All thin stems are A, 898
- All thick branches are C, 898, using two threads

ACTUAL SIZE MOTIFS

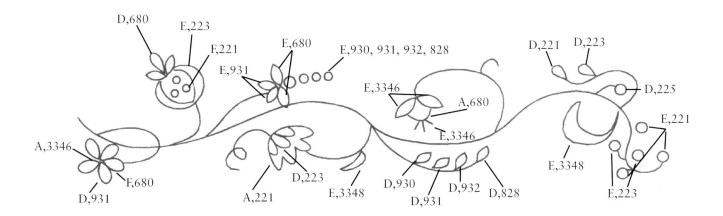

Stitch Diagram: Pillow area and three sides of bedspread on dropped area

PROJECT #4.2
Pastoral Design for Seat Cover
Designed by: Annelle Ferguson

Materials Needed:
>   #60 silk gauze
>   Silk sewing thread/embroidery floss

Stitch Count:
>   87 (w) x 85 (h)

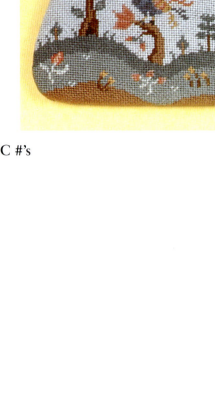

Photo by Anne Day Smith

Color Chart:

Code	Color	Comparable to DMC #'s
◢	Dk. Brown	898
✗	Brown	433
•	Med. Brown	435
○	Dk. Rose	309
▽	Med. Rose	335
Z	Lt. Rose	899
L	Bone	Ecru
✚	Dk. Gold	680
E	Yellow	743
▮	Dk. Green	501
S	Med. Green	503
U	Lt. Green	504
➤	Dk. Blue	792
—	Med. Blue	793
☐	Sky Blue	928

PROJECT #4.3
Carnation Pattern (Repeat design)
Designed by: Annelle Ferguson

Materials Needed:
>   #48 silk gauze
>   DMC embroidery floss

Color Chart:

Code	Color	Comparable to DMC #'s
C	Off-White	746
Z	Vy. Lt. Gold	677
•	Lt. Gold	676
R	Med. Gold	729
S	Vy. Lt. Terra Cotta	758
E	Lt. Terra Cotta	3778
/	Med. Terra Cotta	356
K	Dk. Terra Cotta	3830
×	Med. Green	502
○	Dk. Green	501
□	Vy. Dk. Green (Background)	500

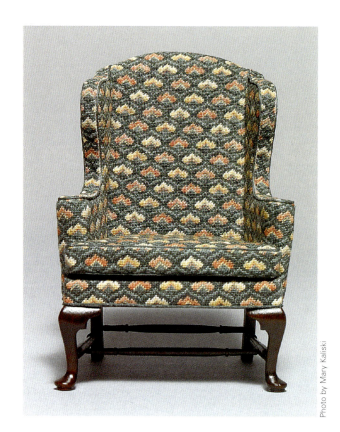

Photo by Mary Kaliski

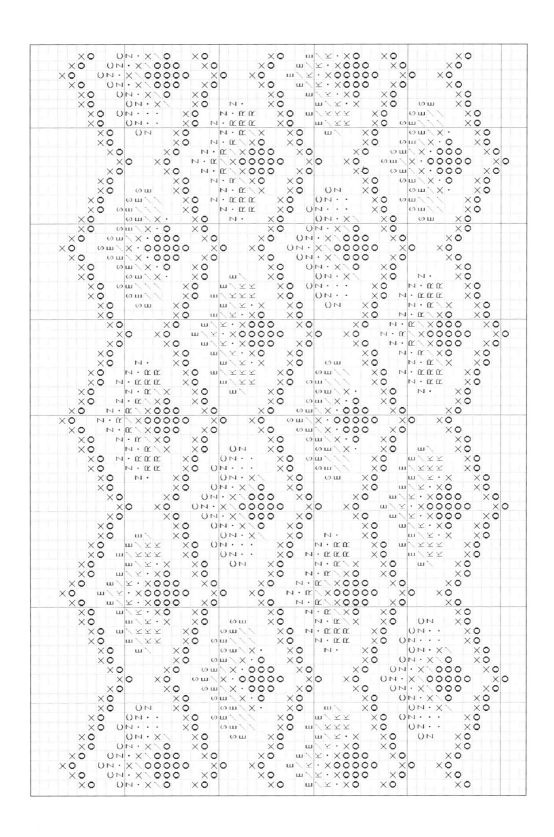

PROJECT #4.3A
Landscaped Chair Back Panel
Designed by: Annelle Ferguson

Materials Needed:
> #48 silk gauze
> DMC embroidery floss

Approx. size of chair:
> 4$\frac{1}{4}$ in. (h) x 3 in. (w) x 1$\frac{7}{8}$ in. (d)

Back panel size: 3$\frac{1}{4}$ in. (h) x 2$\frac{1}{4}$ in. (w)

Color Chart:

Code	Color	Comparable to DMC #'s
●	Vy. Dk. Blue Green	500
o	Dk. Blue Green	501
×	Blue Green	502
8	Med. Blue Green	503
V	Med./Lt. Blue Green	3813
I	Lt. Blue Green	504
▲	Vy. Dk. Terra Cotta	355
K	Dk. Terra Cotta	3839
/	Med. Terra Cotta	356
E	Lt. Terra Cotta	3778
S	Vy. Lt. Terra Cotta	758
▼	Vy. Dk. Grey Green	924
+	Dk. Grey Green	3768
B	Med. Grey Green	926
#	Lt. Grey Green	927
◢	Vy. Dk. Old Gold	3829
I	Dk. Old Gold	680
R	Med. Old Gold	729
·	Lt. Old Gold	676
Z	Vy. Lt. Old Gold - Sky Color	677
C	Off-White	746
◗	Vy. Dk. Brown	838
✖	Dk. Brown	839
▽	Med. Brown	840
➤	Lt. Brown	841
▽	Tan	436
L	Vy. Lt. Tan	738
+	Ecru	
■	Black	3799

SPECIAL INSTRUCTIONS: Fill in blank squares according to colors in pasture

PROJECT #4.4
Field of Flowers
Designed by: Annelle Ferguson

Materials Needed:
 #48 silk gauze
 DMC embroidery floss

Stitch Count:
 73 (w) x 63 (h)

Color Chart:

Code	Color	Comparable to DMC #'s
U	Pale Pink	3770
O	Lt. Peach	758
▽	Med. Peach	3778
•	Dk. Peach	3830
L	Lt. Blue	775
8	Med. Blue	3325
➤	Dk. Blue	334
◤	Dk. Gold	680
V	Yellow	744
Z	Orange	922
×	Lt. Gray Green	3053
S	Med. Gray Green	3052
▮	Dk. Gray Green	3051
╱	Lt. Blue Green	504
E	Med. Blue Green	503
✚	Dk. Blue Green	501
☐	Black (Background)	3799

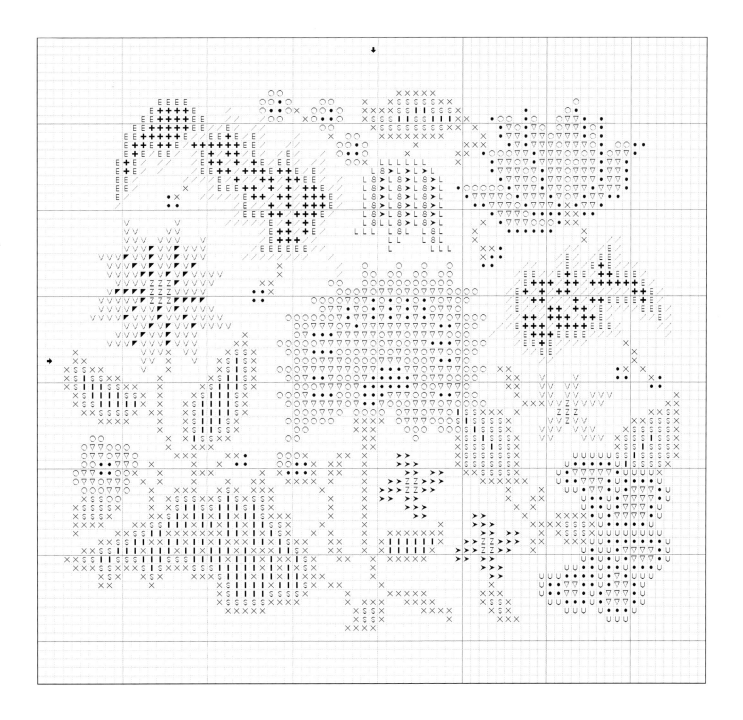

PROJECT #4.5
Game Table Panel
Designed by: Annelle Ferguson

Materials Needed:
>   #48 silk gauze
>   DMC embroidery floss

Stitch Count:
>   73(w) x 69(h)

Game table:
>   2¹/2 in. (h) x 2¹/2 in. (w) 2¹/2 in. (d)

Color Chart:

Code	Color	Comparable to DMC #'s
╱	Vy. Lt. Gold	746
△	Med. Gold	676
•	Dk. Yellow Beige	3045
L	Lt. Yellow Beige	3047
+	Lt. Green	369
×	Med. Green	368
❙	Dk. Rose	3350
○	Med. Rose	3731
−	Lt. Rose	3354
S	Pale Pink	225
Z	White	
➤	Med. Blue	518
☐	Black (Background)	3799

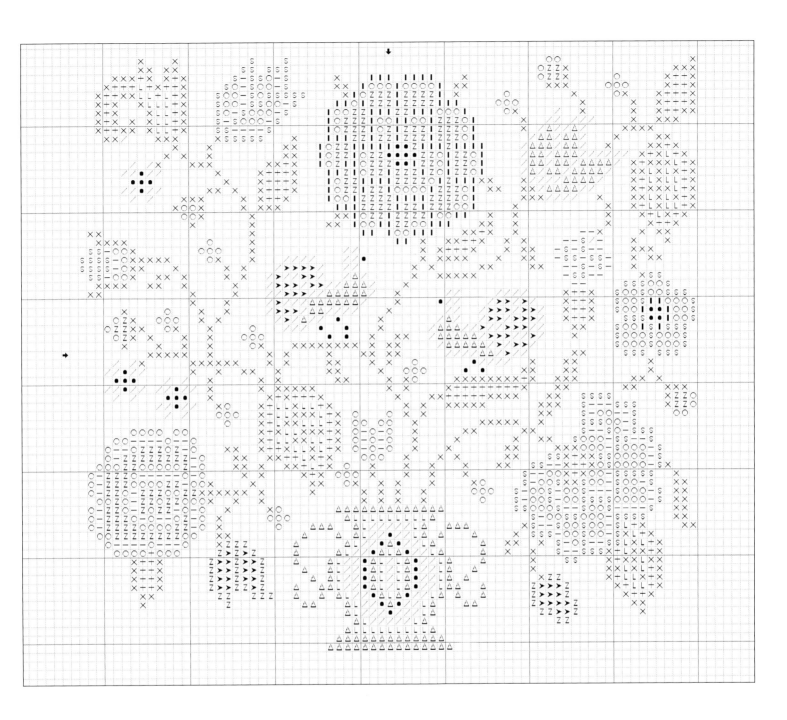

PROJECT #4.6
Floral Spray for Bench Seat
Designed by: Annelle Ferguson

Materials Needed:
> #48 silk gauze
> DMC embroidery floss

Stitch Count:
> 153 (w) x 55 (h)

Color Chart:

Code	Color	Comparable to DMC #'s
➤	Med. Blue	931
△	Lt. Blue	932
/	Med. Green	3052
•	Lt. Green	3053
Z	Pale Green	524
+	Dk. Rose	3350
S	Med. Rose	3731
E	Med. Pink	3326
○	Lt. Pink	819
I	Dk. Gold	729
—	Lt. Gold	677
◿	Orange	922
U	Med. Brown	420
×	Tan	436
V	Off White	746
□	Dk. Blue (Background)	3750

Landscape:

3 Rows	3053
Lower Area	3052

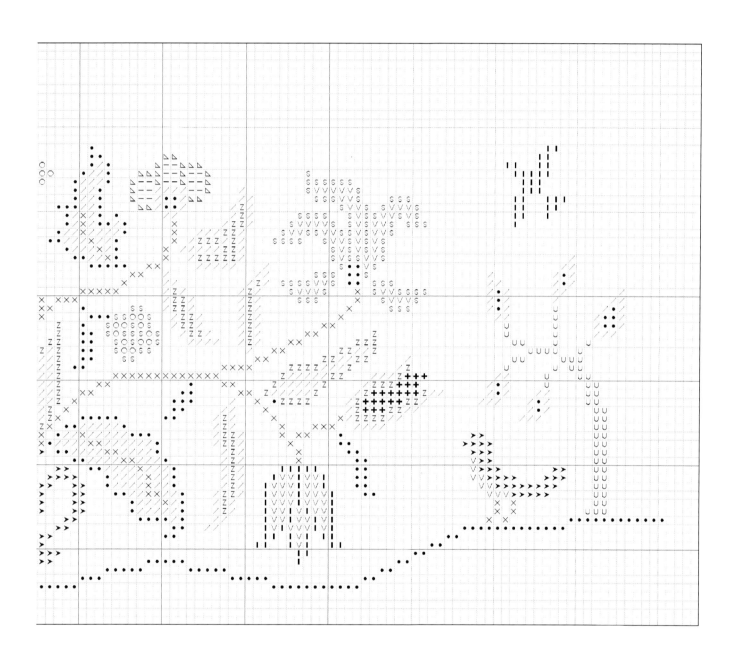

PROJECT #4.7
Small Floral
(for hand-held or table top fire screen)
Designed by: Judith Ohanian

Materials Needed:
> #40 or #48 silk gauze
> DMC embroidery floss

Stitch Count:
> 29 (w) x 29 (h)

Total size: 1³/8 in. (h) x ³/4 in. (w)

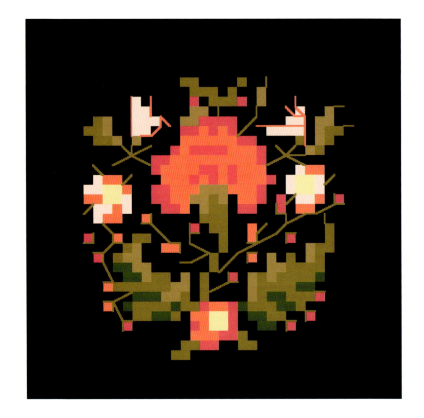

Color Chart:

Code	Color	Comparable to DMC #'s
○	Lt. Salmon	761
—	Med. Salmon	3328
✘	Dk. Salmon (Backstitch color for flower buds)	347
•	Lt. Golden Olive	834
/	Golden Olive	832
S	Med. Golden Olive (Backstitch color for stems)	831
◢	Dk. Fern Green	520
□	Black/Brown (Background)	3371

SPECIAL INSTRUCTIONS: Backstitches are worked after the needlepoint has been completed. The stitches can travel in any direction and can be worked over more than one needlepoint stitch. Pull the stitches only tight enough to lay flat.

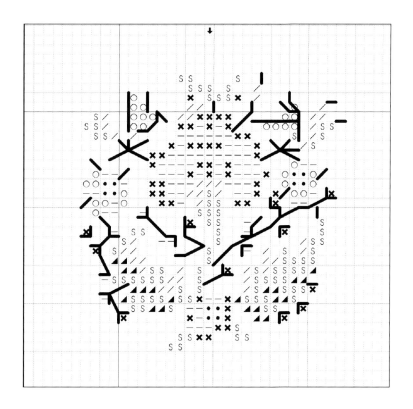

PROJECT #4.8A
Blossoms in Formation
(Repeat Pattern)
Designed by: Annelle Ferguson

Materials Needed:
> #48 or smaller silk gauze
> DMC embroidery floss

Color Chart:

Code	Color	Comparable to DMC #'s
I	Dk. Gold	680
✗	Dk. Pine Green	3362
·	Sky Blue	519
○	Dk. Rose	3731
+	Med. Rose	3733
□	Ecru	

Photo by Mary Kaliski

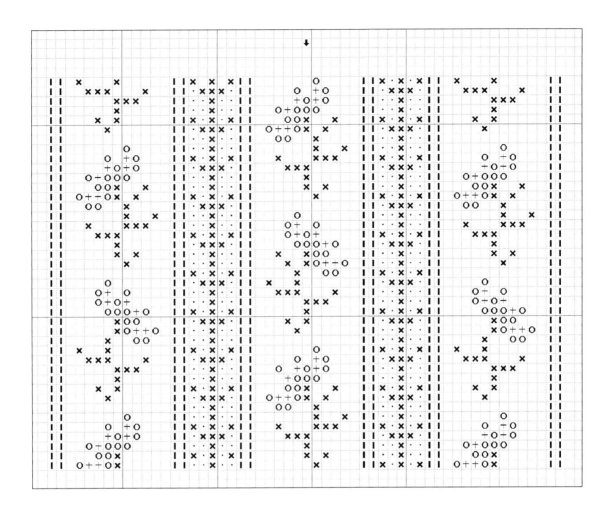

PROJECT #4.8B
Geometric in Nature (Repeat Pattern)
Designed by: Annelle Ferguson

Photo by Mary Kaliski

Materials Needed:
>   #56 or 60 silk gauze
>   Silk sewing thread/embroidery floss

Color Chart:

Code	Color	Comparable to DMC #'s
❙	Dk. Gold	680
○	Med. Gold	676
·	Vy. Lt. Gold	746
✚	Med. Rust	3830
✖	Hunter Green (Background)	3345

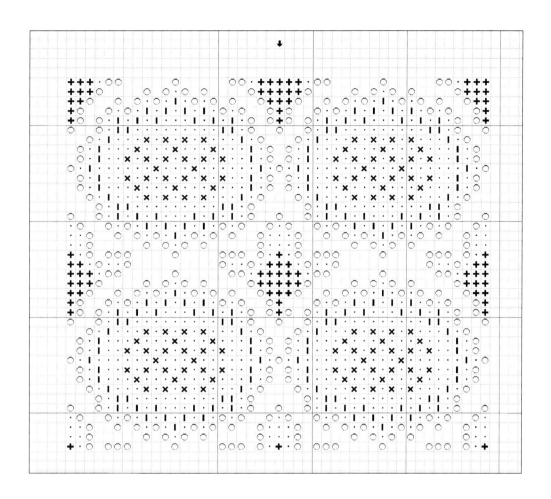

PROJECT #4.8C
Field of Strawberries (Repeat Pattern)
Designed by: Annelle Ferguson

Materials Needed:
>   #48 or smaller silk gauze
>   DMC embroidery floss

Color Chart:

Code	Color	Comparable to DMC #'s
○	Dk. Peach	3830
×	Med. Peach	3778
·	Lt. Peach	3779
/	Med. Green	3053
□	Black (Background)	3799

Photo by Mary Kaliski

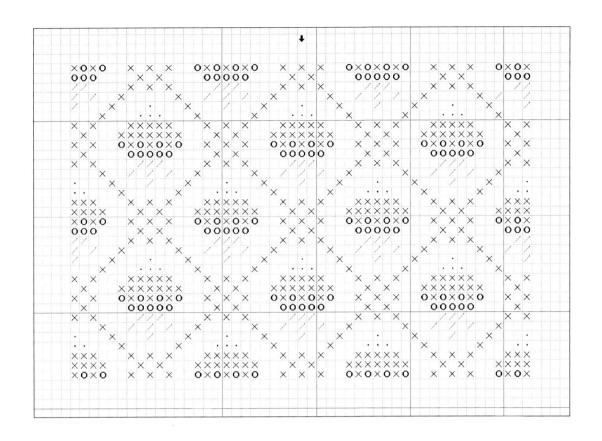

PROJECT #4.8D
Pomegranate (Design for Bargello)
Designed by: Annelle Ferguson

Materials Needed:
>	#48 or smaller silk gauze
>	DMC embroidery floss

Instructions:
Use Bargello stitch (over four threads).

Photo by Mary Kaliski

	Color	Comparable to DMC #'s
Pomegranate outline	Lt. Blue	932
2nd row	Med. Blue	931
3rd row	Dk. Blue	930
4th row	Lt. Rose	223
Center	Dk. Rose	221

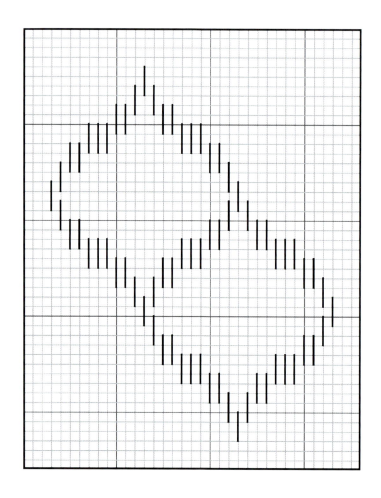

PROJECT #4.9
Colonial Bed rug
Designed by: Clarice Elder

Materials Needed:
  #28 gold linen
  DMC embroidery floss

Stitch Count:
  199 (w) x 192 (h)

Color Chart:

Code	Color	Comparable to DMC #'s
▽	Lt. Brown	434
○	Tan	436
—	Lt. Tan	437
✖	Med. Copper	920
●	Black Brown	3371

Backstitch using the following colors:
  Major vines - 3371
  Other stems - 436

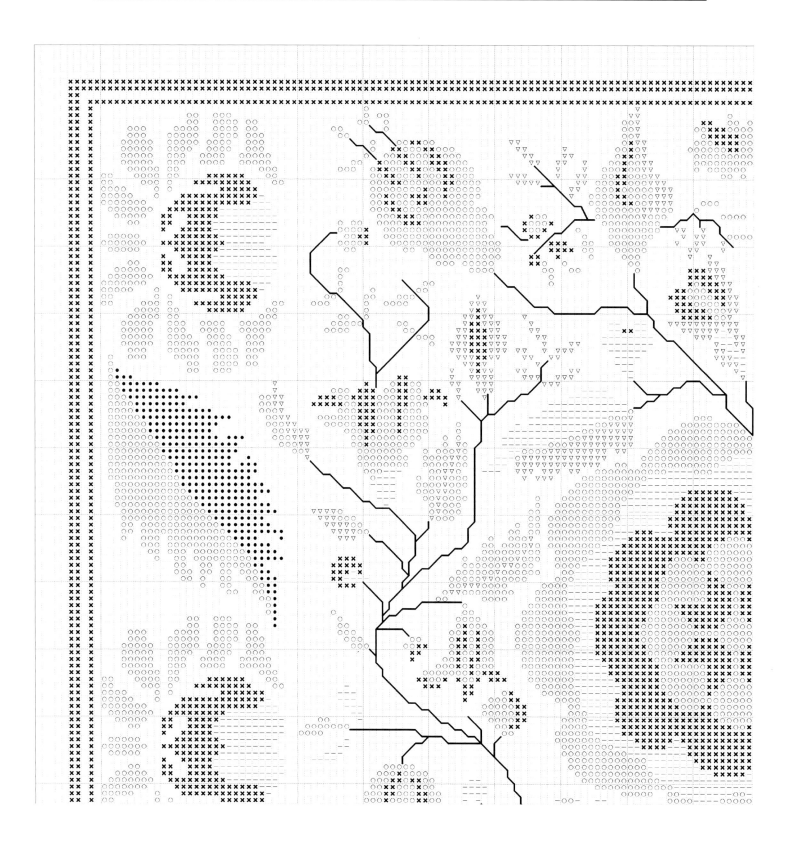

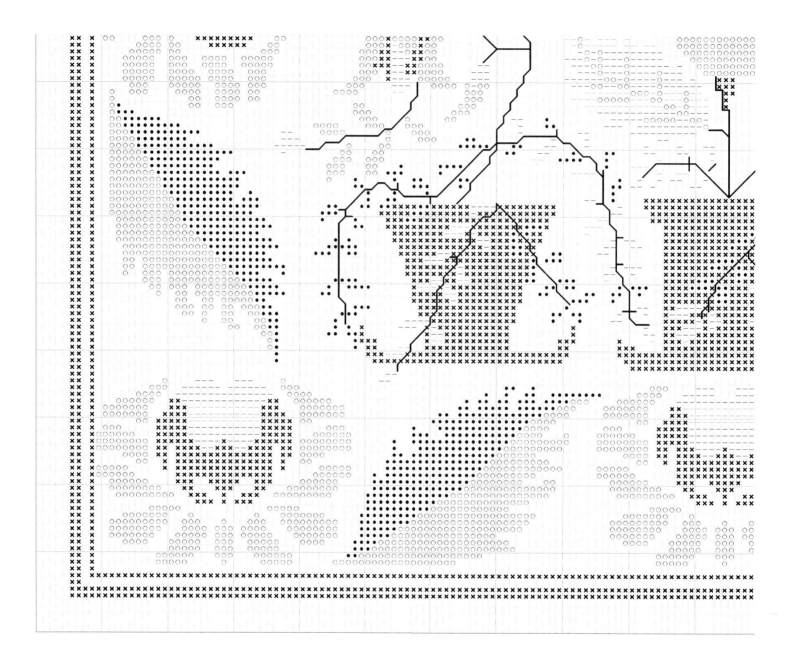

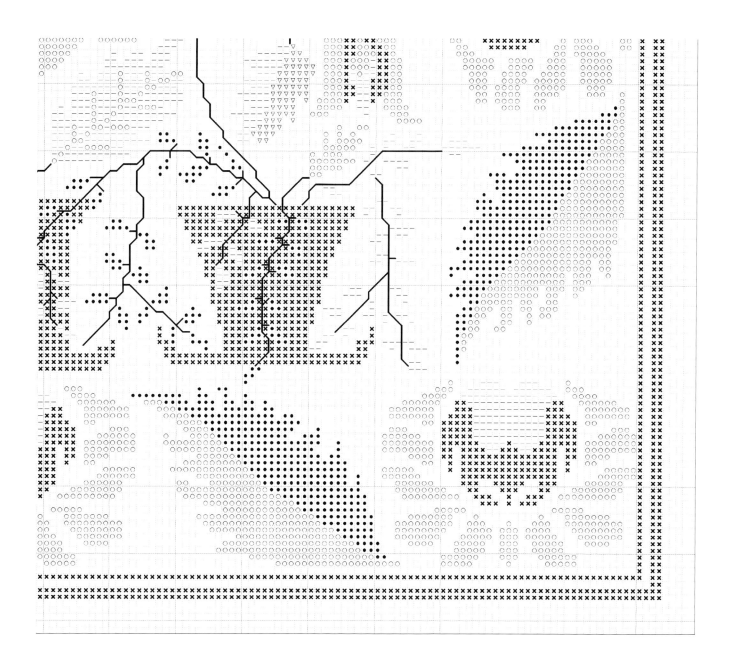

PROJECT #4.10
Pennsylvania Embroidered Picture
Designed by: Annelle Ferguson

Materials Needed:
    #60 silk gauze
    Silk sewing thread/embroidery floss

Stitch Count:
    59 (w) x 71 (h)

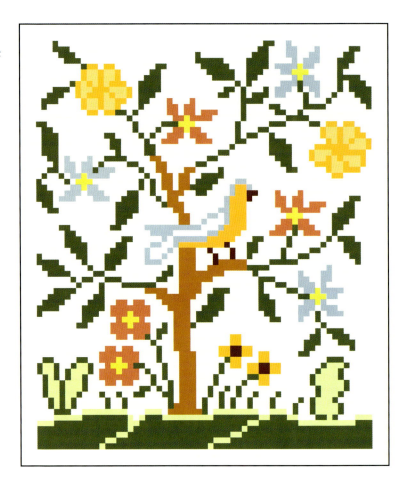

Color Chart:

Code	Color	Comparable to DMC #'s
❙	Med. Brown	420
o	Green	3052
z	Lt. Green	3053
·	Gold	680
▽	Lt. Gold	746
✖	Blue	3768
c	Lt. Blue	927
+	Dk. Salmon	3830
▲	Dk. Yellow	725
/	Tan	437
◢	Dk. Brown	839
□	Ecru (Background)	

18th- and 19th-Century
American Samplers

There is no study that is not capable of delighting us after a little application to it.
—Alexander Pope (1688-1744)

Many American-made samplers from the 18th and 19th centuries have survived and can be found in museums and private collections throughout the United States. The samplers produced between 1700 and 1750 continued to be influenced by English traditions. However, after midcentury the format and composition of samplers changed, thus creating a distinct and unique American art form. From their original purpose of being a record of stitches, samplers became a major part of a young girl's education, where mastering various embroidery stitches was considered a necessary achievement.

Most often, girls would make two kinds of samplers. The first was usually very plain, containing only alphabets and numerals. This style was instrumental in helping children learn their letters and numbers and in training them in the skill of making fine household linens and clothing. Accurate accounts were kept by marking those items with cross-stitched initials, numbers and date. Instruction in plain sewing, along with learning cooking and household management, was essential for young girls who would someday have their own homes and families and needed to learn the skills required in caring for them. For the middle-class child, this very often constituted her entire education.

The second, and more elaborate samplers were made under tutelage at a girls academy or seminary. Parents who could afford it sent their daughters to a boarding or day school to learn the "accomplishments of proper young ladies." Instruction in fancy embroidery was part of the curriculum, which also included music, dancing, English and French. The decorative samplers from this period have survived in great numbers because they were intended to be preserved. Upon completion, they were framed and usually hung in a prominent place in the family home.

It was in the female academies, flourishing at the end of the 18th century, that fine needle arts were taught. The designs still contained one or more alphabets, numerals, verses, the maker's name, age or date of birth and date of work. Also included were such elements as landscapes, animals, people and wide floral borders. After the Revolutionary War, better educations were more prevalent. However, American society continued to place the same value on embroidery for girls as did the English. Therefore, the sampler prospered until the mid-19th century.

Linen continued to be a background fabric. From 1798 to 1832, a dark olive-green ground, called linsey-woolsey, was used for samplers. It was woven using a combination of vertical blue-green linen threads and horizontal yellow-green wool threads. Silk and linen were the most popular embroidery threads used on samplers. Imported threads and dyes were expensive, resulting in a limited choice of colors. Threads were also frequently home-dyed. Silk yarns and fabrics were easily obtained after the Revolutionary War when America began trading with China.

All samplers at a particular school usually shared the same design elements, thanks to the influence of the individual teacher. Professional patterns were available, but it was the instructor who was responsible for designing the majority of patterns and supervising her charges in the art of fine stitchery. In *Samplers and Samplermakers*, Mary Jaene Edmonds writes of the schoolmistress: "The act of designing samplers became a creative outlet for her. She expressed her individuality by creating the format and embellishing the bands of lettering with flowery sprays, landscapes and people in elaborate costumes of the period. Thus the schoolmistress assumed the role of folk artist and her exquisite designs for needlework on linen are a form of American folk art."

Many of the teachers who established schoolgirl academies during the second half of the 18th century were from England. Some were young unmarried women, having just completed their own schooling. Others were widows or older "spinsters" needing to earn a living. The duration of the school largely depended upon the founder. If she married or remarried, the school usually closed unless she was in need of additional income. The schoolmistresses often advertised in local newspapers stressing their skills at fine needlework, and their abilities to provide a genteel education for young ladies.

The earliest known schools emerged along the eastern seaboard. Although a specific teacher and location of the school is unknown, a group of samplers worked in Boston during the 1720s are generally known as the Adam and Eve samplers. These are in the same style as the English band samplers. The base of the long and narrow shape shows Adam and Eve standing on either side of a tree with a snake coiled around it, surrounded by various animals and birds. The top is filled with rows of borders and alphabets.

An increase in population in Massachusetts contributed to the opening of a number of private schools for girls after mid-18th century. Some of the most outstanding groups of samplers were worked in Salem and Newbury/Newburyport. A very distinct collection of samplers was produced in Newbury and Newburyport over a 60 year period. From about 1750, the various styles are recognized by the same floral band pattern, as seen on earlier English work, within a trefoil border. Designs from the school run by Sarah Stivours rival those from Boston. She taught in Salem from 1778 until 1794. Schools in Danvers, Haverhill and Marblehead produced exceptional groups of New England samplers in the 18th century. It was not until the early 19th century that a recognizable school of work emerged from Plymouth, this first New England town.

Rhode Island samplers convey a certain charm not found on other American schoolgirl embroideries. Distinctive features originating on early Newport samplers continued in various forms to other areas of Rhode Island in later years. Samplers from the last half of the century are similar in their layered format and wide floral borders. The figures that randomly appear in various scenes are known as the "frolicking people."

Photo by Mary and Tom Kaliski

Full-size Sarah Lowell sampler, 1750, Boston, Massachusetts. Inscription: "Sarah Lowell her Sampler Wrought in 1750." Sarah was born April 10, 1738 to Boston merchant Ebenezer Lowell and his wife, Mary Reed. She was married December 6, 1759 to Edward Blanchard, had 12 children and died August 24, 1792. From the collection of Glee Krueger.

Philadelphia sampler, 1½ x 1¾ inches, Project 5.4

Sarah Lowell sampler, Project 5.2

Rhode Island sampler, Project 5.3

Adam & Eve sampler, 1 x 2 inches, Project 5.1

Two notable Newport samplers, worked a generation apart, are those by mother and daughter, Sarah Rogers and Mary Balch. Sarah completed her sampler in 1746 at age 11. Like earlier samplers from this period, the floral band patterns indicate an English style. Sarah married Timothy Balch in 1757 and Mary was one of their six children. Mary, born in 1762, made her sampler in 1773 when she was also 11 years old. These two samplers remained in the Balch family, having been passed down from generation to generation. They were discovered in California in 1979 when a family member learned of their historical value. Both samplers were given to the Rhode Island Historical Society.

Sarah Rogers Balch was widowed shortly after the family moved from Newport to Providence in 1776. Mary, at an early age, assumed a great deal of financial responsibility for the family, and in 1785 opened what became the most renowned schoolgirl academy in Rhode Island. Designs created under her instruction at the Providence school are the best known and probably the most striking of all 18th-century, American-made samplers. Mary's students individually combined architectural structures with landscapes, figures and animals in a two- or three-layered format, framed by an archway. Borders were florals growing from identical urns. Stitches used, as in the majority of 18th-century designs, were cross-stitch, tent, satin, and stem or outline stitch. "Let Virtue be a guide to thee" was a favorite verse used on the Balch school samplers, or sentiments such as, "May spotless innocence and truth my every action guide and guard my unexperienced youth from arrogance and pride." The academy was in operation until its founder's death in 1811.

The death of George Washington in 1799 is said to be the inspiration for the popular mourning embroideries done by New England schoolgirls. The many memorial prints were sources of design. Not all designs were dedicated to Washington; many were made in memory of family members. These embroideries continued into the 1820s. The designs included urns, monuments and willow trees embroidered in silk on silk fabric.

Pennsylvania Quaker sampler, Project 5.7

Samplers continued to flourish in New England girls academies until the middle of the 19th century. A distinguishable group of samplers was created by schoolgirls in the Canterbury, New Hampshire, area from 1786 to 1833. Characteristic in the lower section is the centered basket from which flowers, outlined in black, emerge. Samplers from the Dover and Portsmouth areas are identifiable by their use of lindsey-woolsey ground. The samplers worked between 1803 and 1820 in the Portland, Maine, region have either genealogical information or alphabets and verses surrounded by a wide rose-vine border.

Maine sampler, Project 5.5

Early settlements in Pennsylvania were established by a variety of nationalities and religions and most schoolgirls produced work influenced by their homeland. The greatest number of settlers were from England and the majority of them were Quakers. The first girls schools were in operation by 1727. The most notable samplers from this period are those worked between 1725 and 1740. A sampler worked by Ann Marsh in 1727 is one of several that closely resembles the English band patterns. The floral band motifs alternate with long verses and are enclosed with a stylized border.

Ann was born in England but migrated to America with her parents as a young child. It was Ann's mother, Elizabeth Marsh, schoolmistress, who established the

Mourning embroidery, Project 5.6

needlework styles from the 1720s to the 1790s. Ann, also a teacher for much of her long life, continued the traditions set by her mother. She never married and probably began her teaching career with her mother. She instructed the daughters of many prominent Philadelphians between 1772 and 1789, and died in 1797. Several pieces of her work are in the collection of the Chester County Historical Society.

By late 1799, the Quakers had opened a school outside Philadelphia. Called Westtown, it was a boarding school for both girls and boys and is still in operation today. An equal education was offered for both sexes, except that the girls had instruction in needlework and the boys had more instruction in mathematics. The Westtown school was under the influence of Ackworth School in England. By 1800, Westtown samplers and samplers from other Quaker schools reflected the same designs found on Ackworth samplers. A first needleworked piece for Quaker girls was often a darning sampler, which taught a useful skill for mending fabrics. Typical samplers embroidered at these schools were worked in black silk on a linen ground. A pious verse was surrounded by a vine and leaf scroll border.

During the first half of the 19th century, Quaker samplers became more decorative. Students stitched their names and the date in the center, encircled by scattered motifs of fruit baskets, flowers and birds or animals. Stuffed globe samplers have also survived from the Westtown schools. They were very similar to the English-made map samplers. The continents, longitude and latitude lines were outlined in silk threads. On silk ground other details were painted.

The embroidery of the early Pennsylvania German settlers closely followed their European traditions. The samplers contained a series of motifs scattered around a borderless squared shape in a more or less orderly fashion. The patterns used were later found on the delicate hand towels the girls would be expected to embroider.

Throughout the last half of the 18th century and first half of the 19th century, schools continued to be opened in eastern Pennsylvania by various German sects, each continuing their traditional styles of needlework. A highly reputable school, first founded in Germantown in the early 1740s by Moravian Church leaders and followers, was permanently moved to Bethlehem in 1749. It became known as the Moravian Seminary for Young Ladies. The school was opened to non-Moravian girls in 1786 and was attended by the daughters of some of the country's most prominent families. The girls received intensive instruction in a wide range of needlework skills along with lessons in subject matters usually reserved for boys—arithmetic, geography, history and botany as well as reading and writing in English and German. The school remains today as the Moravian Academy.

Quaker schools were also common in Delaware during the late 18th century and early 19th century. Samplers from Maryland and other Delaware schools were worked between 1811 and 1835 and a small number of pieces were worked in Washington between 1810 and 1813. In private schools existing in Ohio after 1803, the styles were influenced by Quaker and German settlers.

Southern samplers exist, but in small numbers. The Moravians of Salem, North Carolina, opened Salem Academy in 1804. The needlework produced there is very much like Pennsylvania Moravian work. Tutors were often hired to teach children at home and more often, young girls were taught stitchery by their mothers. Family records indicate that a number of girls from the South attended schoolgirl academies in New England.

After 1840, sampler making as an educational exercise began to decline. More public schools were opening in the North and a higher degree of learning was sought for girls.

Chapter 5 *Projects*
18th- & 19-Century American Samplers

All projects are for personal use only. They may not be stitched and sold for profit.

PROJECT #5.1
Early 18th Century Adam & Eve Sampler

Designed by: Nancy Sturgeon

Materials Needed:
    #48 Silk gauze
    DMC embroidery floss

Stitch Count:
    47 (w) x 91 (h)
    Finished size: 1 in. (w) x 2 in. (h)

Color Chart:

Code	Color	Comparable to DMC #'s
△	Red	356
✖	Dk. Green	520
+	Med. Green	522
○	Brown	610
❘	Gold	729
➤	Charcoal	844
●	Blue	926
S	Flesh	3773
☐	Ecru (Background)	

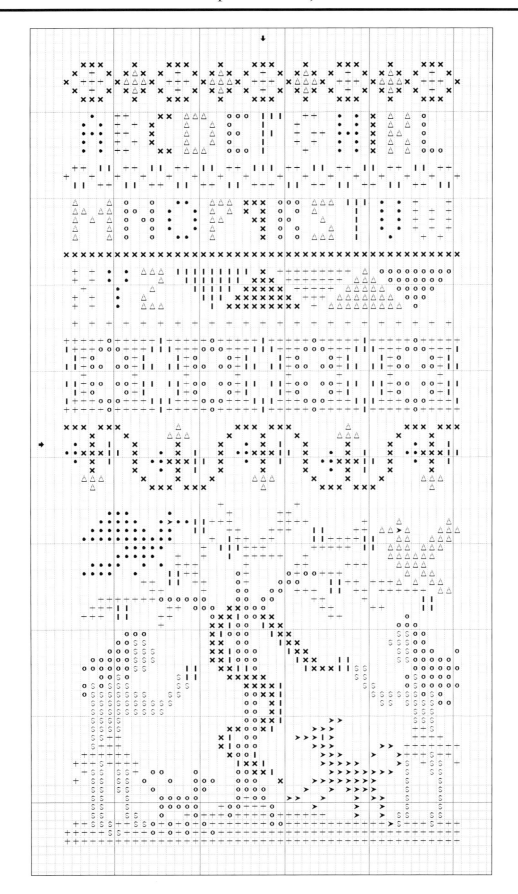

PROJECT #5.2
Sarah Lowell Sampler
Designed by: Annelle Ferguson

Materials Needed:
   #60 (or smaller) silk gauze
   Silk sewing thread/silk embroidery floss

Stitch Count:
   81 (w) x 103 (h)

Color Chart:

Code	Color	Comparable to DMC #'s
✖	Dk. Forest Green	3051
S	Med. Forest Green	3052
❙	Dk. Gold	680
▽	Med. Gold	676
●	Med. Rust	3830
○	Dk. Teal Blue	924
+	Med. Teal Blue	926
E	Lt. Teal Blue	927
☐	Ecru (Background)	

PROJECT #5.3
Rhode Island Sampler (c. 1795)
Designed by: Annelle Ferguson

Materials Needed:
>#60 silk gauze
>Silk sewing thread/embroidery floss

Stitch Count:
>89 (w) x 97 (h)

Color Chart:

Code	Color	Comparable to DMC #'s
o	Dk. Peach	356
▲	Black	844
✕	Ecru	
·	Med. Blue	3755
➤	Dk. Blue	322
▽	Brown	435
C	Gold	729
+	Dk. Gold	3045
V	Med. Green	3053
—	Flesh	950
/	White	
I	Lt. Sky Blue (Background) Behind Cherubs	3756
✕	Ecru Behind Verse (Background)	
2	Ivory Behind House (Background)	842
☐	Dk. Brown (Border Background)	839

Circled code indicates filling in background with that color.

PROJECT #5.4
Philadelphia Sampler (c. 1730)
Designed by: Annelle Ferguson

Materials Needed:
> #60 silk gauze
> Silk sewing thread/embroidery floss

Stitch Count:
> 85 (w) x 107 (h)
> Finished size: 1½ in. x 1¾ in.

Color Chart:

Code	Color	Comparable to DMC #'s
○	Med. Green	3052
❙	Dk. Rust	355
•	Med. Rust	356
E	Lt. Peach	758
✕	Med. Blue	926
▼	Dk. Gold	680
☐	Off-White (Background)	822

PROJECT #5.5
18th-Century Maine Samper
Designed by: Annelle Ferguson

Materials Needed:
  #60 silk gauze
  Silk sewing thread/embroidery floss

Stitch Count:
  83 (w) x 103 (h)

Color Chart:

Code	Color	Comparable to DMC #'s
I	Med. Gold	729
✕	Black	844
▽	Med. Blue	334
○	Lt. Green	3053
•	White	
S	Lt. Copper	922
▲	Dk. Green	3051
✚	Brown	420
╱	Taupe	642
Z	Lt. Sky Blue	828
L	Med. Green	3052
—	Lt. Gold	676
☐	Dk. Taupe (Background)	840

Circled code indicates filling in background with that color.

PROJECT #5.6
19th-Century Mourning Embroidery

Designed by: Annelle Ferguson

Materials Needed:
        #48 (or smaller) silk gauze
        DMC embroidery floss

Color Chart:

Code	Color	Comparable to DMC #'s
✚	Dk. Gray	318
V	Med. Gray	415
O	Ecru	
△	Brown	429
▼	Dk. Brown	869
✖	Dk. Green	937
•	Med. Green	470
E	Lt. Green	472
S	Tan	422
➤	Rust	3830
❙	Dk. Teal Blue	519
Z	Med. Teal Blue	3761
C	Lt. Teal Blue	747
	Pale Blue/Green (Sky)	928

(Alternate 937, 470, 472 & 422 for landscape)

Circled code indicates filling in background with that color.

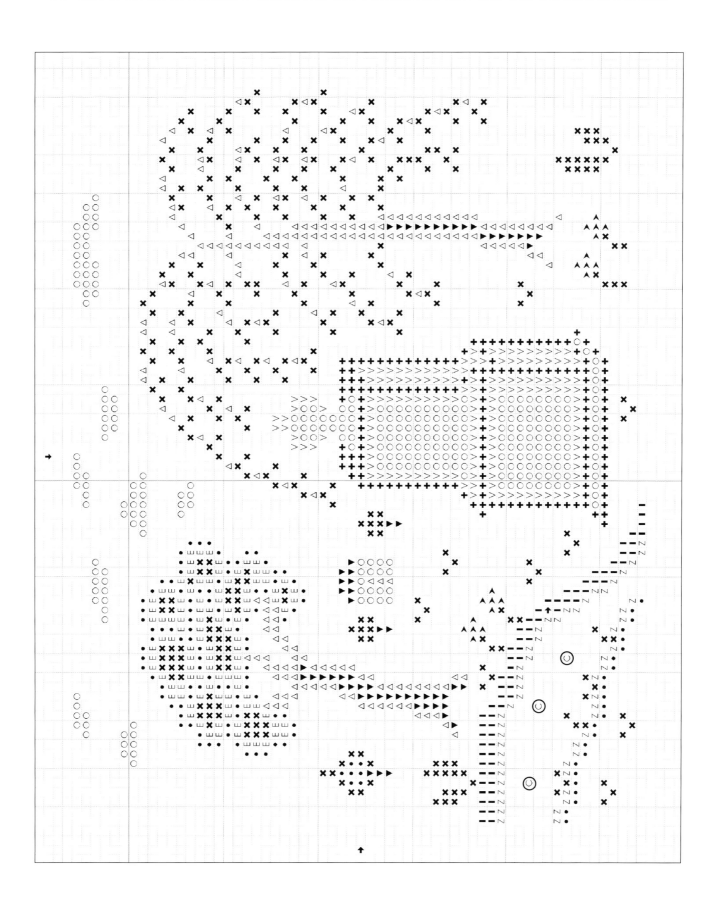

PROJECT #5.7
19th-Century Quaker Sampler
Designed by: Pat Tulski

Materials Needed:
> #48 silk gauze
> DMC embroidery floss

Stitch Count:
> 59 (w) x 81 (h)

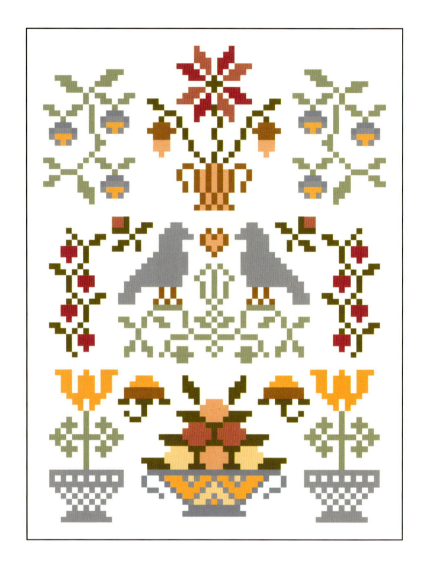

Color Chart:

Code	Color	Comparable to DMC #'s
╱	Lt. Rose	3722
•	Dk. Rose	221
▼	Dk. Green	3051
△	Med. Green	3052
✕	Med. Blue	931
○	Dk. Blue	930
E	Med. Gold	3828
✚	Dk. Gold	869
V	Lt. Tan	738
S	Med. Tan	436

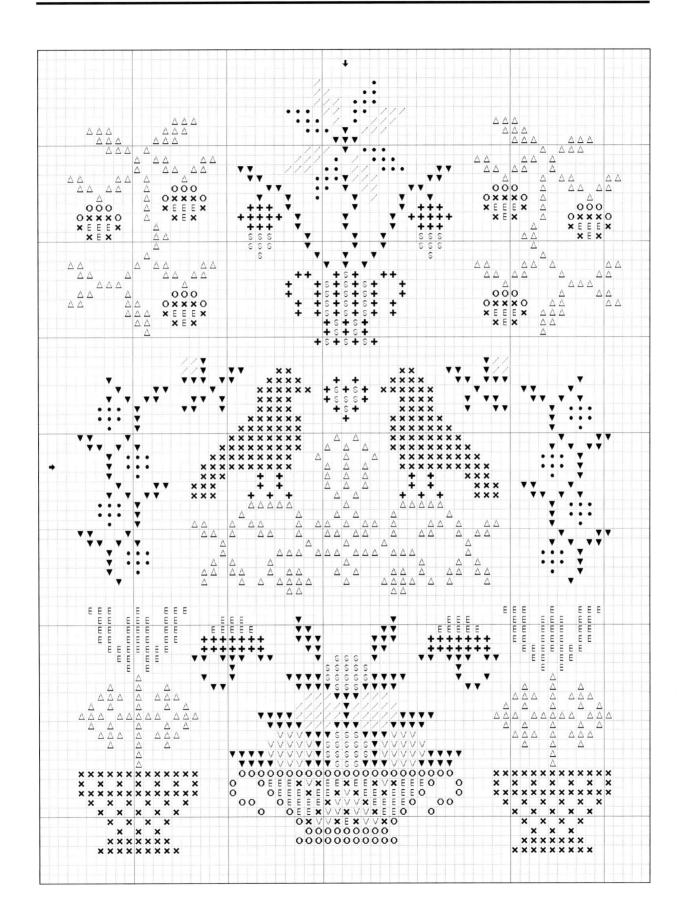

Chapter 6

19th-Century
English and American Needlework

Great designs are not accomplished without enthusiasm of some sort.
—Christian Nestell Bovee (1820-1904)

The 19th century is generally referred to as the Victorian Age, due in part to the long
reign of Queen Victoria in England. She ascended the throne in 1837 at the young age
of 18 and ruled for 64 years. It was during those decades that England and America witnessed
numerous economic, political and social changes.

At the beginning of the 19th century, the schoolgirl academies in America and England were
well attended by daughters from prosperous families. Little change was seen in the originality
and creativity of samplers during the first quarter of the century. Silk embroidered pictures were
widely produced in the schoolroom. The various designs included charming settings with children dressed as shepherds and shepherdesses, historical or religious scenes, and the ever-popular

mourning embroideries that noted the passing of a loved one. By midcentury, scholastic subjects were stressed rather than embroidery, but young women continued to learn basic needlework at home and from the numerous books now being published on the subject.

In the English schools attended by working-class children, samplers were considered necessary training for girls who would eventually enter into service with a family. As a domestic servant, she might be responsible for making and repairing household furnishings and clothing. Numerals and alphabets in various sizes and scripts were recorded in cross-stitch with border patterns and moral verses often being added.

However, not all young girls were enrolled in school. In *Samplers, Five Centuries of a Gentle Craft*, Anne Sebba writes, "In spite of the new interest in education, school attendance was low throughout most of the century. Times were hard, and for most urban and rural children it was more important that they earned money sweeping chimneys, hauling coal or pulling turnips." In 1870, an Education Act was passed to ensure a national educational system.

In the second quarter of the century, a new style of needlework erupted that would change

Full-size English sampler, stitched by Sarah Ann Smith, age 12, at St. Andrew's School, dated December 8, 1862. From the collection of Barbara Cosgrove. Barbara used this design to create her miniature sampler, Project 6.1.

Photo by Barbara Cosgrove

the very nature of the craft itself. For over a fifty-year period, European and American needleworkers were consumed by a new technique for canvas work called Berlin woolwork. The affluent, leisured ladies of comfortable means engaged in this new style of embroidery with great enthusiasm. A new middle class had emerged and most middle-class women also pursued this new method of stitchery. From about 1830 to 1870, the rage for Berlin woolwork surpassed all other types of needlework. By midcentury, a new industry had been created for its production.

In 1804, Mr. A. Philipson, a printmaker in Berlin, Germany, published the first colored patterns on checkered paper. The first patterns were hand colored, square by square. Each square on the graph paper represented one stitch on the canvas. The design could then be needlepointed on a canvas ground, using the tent stitch and wool thread. Philipson's patterns were the

Anne Chauvin's needlework shows various examples of Berlin wool work. (*Miniature Collector*, April 1997, p. 35)

first to indicate to the stitcher exactly how to achieve an end result. The earlier 18th-century patterns were only outlines. Choices on color, shading and stitch technique were left entirely to the desire of the embroiderer. In 1810, another Berliner, Mr. L. W. Wittich, started producing patterns and soon led the market in what would eventually be referred to as Berlin woolwork designs. Other print publishers eventually followed suit.

The patterns gradually spread outside Germany and by 1820 had reached England. In 1831, a Mr. Wilks began importing the patterns, and the materials for working them, in large quantities for his shop on Regent Street in London. Fourteen-thousand patterns had been printed by 1840, all hand-colored by an array of workers employed by the numerous publishers in America, England and other European countries. Much later in the 19th century, printing the charts in color replaced the hand-colored designs. Ladies' monthly magazines began printing patterns about 1860. *The Englishwoman's Domestic Magazine* published instructions and patterns. *Godey's Lady's Book*, published in Philadelphia, was America's most fashionable magazine and printed its patterns in color. In America, Berlin wool work peaked in 1856, but continued its popularity for 30 more years.

The first Berlin patterns were worked entirely in tent stitch using Merino wool yarn manufactured in Germany. Merino wool was finer than worsted wool and as soft as crewel wool. Worsted and crewel wools had been predominate in the previous century. Most colors were quite vivid and flamboyant. After 1850, dark colors, especially black, were being used to fill in backgrounds. An evenly-woven cotton canvas replaced the fine silk canvas that had been used before 1820.

Subject matter for the Berlin patterns evolved from a variety of sources. Philipson's first designs were flowers gathered in wreaths and bouquets. Floral designs were the most popular, often displayed in large clusters of contemporary flowers in bright and bold colors. The many patterns containing birds were often inspired by such books on birds as Audubon's *Birds of America* or Gould's *Birds of Australia*. Parrots were a particularly favorite specie included in the Berlin patterns.

Many designs were copies of famous paintings. Since there were no copyright laws, permission was not necessary for reproducing such works. In 1851, at the Great Exhibition in Britain, there were six embroidered adaptations of Leonardo da Vinci's *The Last Supper* displayed, as well as copies of other famous paintings. Queen Victoria's pets were of special

Photo by Mary and Tom Kaliski

Berlin-style floral chair seat designed by Duffy Wineman for a Linda LaRoche chair. King Charles spaniel designed by Annelle Ferguson. Projects 6.3, 6.5.

Photo by Jason Getzan

Berlin wool work-style seat pattern of parrot sitting on a branch, a very popular needlework design during the Victorian era. Round footstool designed and stitched by Annelle Ferguson, worked on #60 silk gauze.

interest. Numerous patterns derived from Sir Edwin Landseer's paintings of the royal pets. King Charles spaniels or cats lounging on tasseled cushions were favorite scenes. The royal family and other historical figures were included in the thousands of patterns offered in Berlin woolwork patterns.

Available patterns kept women constantly busy with handiwork and gave them an opportunity to adorn every practical object, and some impractical ones, with needlework. Furnishing rooms with matching sets of furniture was no longer stylish. Odd chairs, sofas and stools were being placed in the Victorian parlor along with marble-topped tables, carved sideboards, tiered whatnot shelves and other furnishings to create the cluttered appearance so fashionable during this period.

Floral designs were used for chair seats, sofas, footstools and piano benches. The seats of the lady's rose-carved, balloon-back side chair were favorites to embellish with Berlin wool work. Lively bird designs were found on pictures, pole and banner screens. Lambrequins covered mantels and window frames. Cushions and pillows were decorated with domestic pets. Other household items such as bellpulls, ladies' bags, men's slippers and pincushions were covered with Berlin woolwork, all contributing to the Victorian's desire to decorate their homes.

Embroidered picture *Lady at Tree*, designed by Annelle Ferguson, stitched on #60 silk gauze in the style of Berlin woolwork taken from famous paintings. Toy and Miniature Museum of Kansas City collection.

Photo by Annelle Ferguson

Canvas-worked carpets continued to be made in the 19th century, remaining as popular as they had been in previous centuries. The Berlin style of using vibrant colors in floral and geometrical designs applied as well to carpets in the Victorian period. However, changes were made in the construction of the carpets. Specific designs for carpets were printed on individual canvas squares. The required number of completed squares were then joined together and finished off with a stylized border surrounding the whole carpet. Often, groups of people would work together on such a project, with each

Photo by Mary and Tom Kaliski

Bellpull designed by Anne Chauvin. Project 6.4.

Photo by Mary and Tom Kaliski

Berlin wool work-style floral carpet designed by Shirlee Greenberg. Lambrequin designed by Judith Kaelin. Projects 6.7, 6.8.

person working on separate canvas squares.

Children's samplers continued to be made and were influenced by Berlin woolwork. By 1830 they were worked on woolen cloths with wool yarns. These samplers have not survived as well as those worked on fine linen. Around 1820, a different style of sampler was worked on perforated cardboard or Bristol board. Made of a special grade of card-

Adaptation of 1862 English sampler designed by Barbara Cosgrove. Bristol board-style sampler designed by Erma Scrimgeour. Projects 6.1, 6.9.

board with small holes placed in rows, Bristol board could be used in the same manner as canvas. Small items such as bookmarks as well as large framed pieces with religious and homey mottoes such as "Rock of Ages Cleft for Me" or "No Place Like Home" were produced on the Bristol board. Bristol board samplers remained popular until early in the 20th century.

By the 1870s, the quality of Berlin woolwork declined. The Berlin era was fading and was replaced by Art Needlework. Specialized groups and organizations were forming, seeking ways to improve the quality of embroidery design and technique. The Royal School of Art Needlework was founded in England in 1872 for this purpose and was promoted by leaders of the Arts and Crafts Movement, such as William Morris. He and other artists were often commissioned to provide embroidery designs for the ladies employed by the school.

William Morris-style wall hanging designed by Clarice Elder. Chair seat designed by Anne Chauvin. Side chair by Betty Valentine. Projects 6.10, 6.11.

William Morris (1834-1896), English designer, artist, poet, and social reformer, devoted his career to reviving the ideals of craftsmanship and returning to the achievements of creative work found in previous centuries. The firm of Morris, Marshall, Faulkner & Co., was founded in London in 1861 to design and produce such articles as wallpapers, furniture, and textiles. Later, in 1875, the firm had become Morris & Co., under his sole direction.

Morris had a special interest in embroidery and early in his career researched the techniques found in 17th-century crewelwork. In order to learn the various stitches, he would often pick out the threads of early embroidered pieces. Having mastered the different stitches and materials used, he designed such articles as wall hangings and coverlets for his firm. Morris's patterns are easily identified by their flowing lines and their bird and flower designs in soft, muted colors.

In 1885, Morris's daughter took over the embroidery section of the firm. May Morris (1862-

1938) was as interested in embroidery as her father and chose to closely follow his techniques and methods. She contributed her knowledge to various publications on embroidery and in 1893, her book, *Decorative Needlework*, was published. May's designing and embroidering skills contributed to the success of Morris & Co. late in the 19th and early 20th centuries. Her own designs of wall hangings, screens, and cushion covers were evidence of her artistic accomplishments.

Embroidery has always been used as a means to decorate homes and personal belongings. After the Industrial Revolution, machines produced neccessities, and the homemaker made fewer items in the home. It was no longer imperative to produce fine needleworked articles for furnishings or for costumes. However, throughout the 20th century, the art of hand needlework remained a favorite and popular avocation.

Sue Bakker needlework design based on William Morris weavings. Detail taken from and in style of the *Forest Tapestry* wall hanging, dated 1887. Neale Albert collection.

Peacock designed by Sharon Garmize, fire screen stand by David Booth. Slippers by Bobbie Schoonmaker. Projects 6.2 & 6.6

This is a detail shot of the full-size antique side chair shown on the opening page of this chapter. It had belonged ot the grandmother of current owner, Duffy Wineman.

19th-Century English and American Needlework

All projects are for personal use only. They may not be stitched and sold for profit.

PROJECT #6.1
1862 English Sampler
Designed by: Barbara Cosgrove

Materials Needed:
> #60 silk gauze
> Silk sewing thread/embroidery floss

Stitch Count:
> 79 (w) x 97 (h)

Color Chart:

Code	Color	Comparable to DMC #'s
✖	Dk. Hunter Green	895
○	Dk. Golden Beige	3045
☐	Off-White	822

PROJECT #6.2
Peacock Panel
Designed by: Sharon Garmize

Materials Needed:
  #40/48 silk gauze
   DMC embroidery floss

Stitch Count:
  43 (w) x 55 (h)

Color Chart:

Code	Color	Comparable to DMC #'s
•	Dk. Blue	930
o	Med. Blue	931
Z	Lt. Blue	932
✖	Dk. Rose	221
S	Rust	301
➤	Dk. Gold	680
I	Emerald Green	561
T	Turquoise	3766 (or 807)
E	Med. Gold	676
▼	Branch Green	3011
/	Yellow/Green	472
C	Leaf Green	3052
L	Dk. Dusty Rose	3350
✚	Med. Dusty Rose	3733
□	Lt. Blue (Background)	928

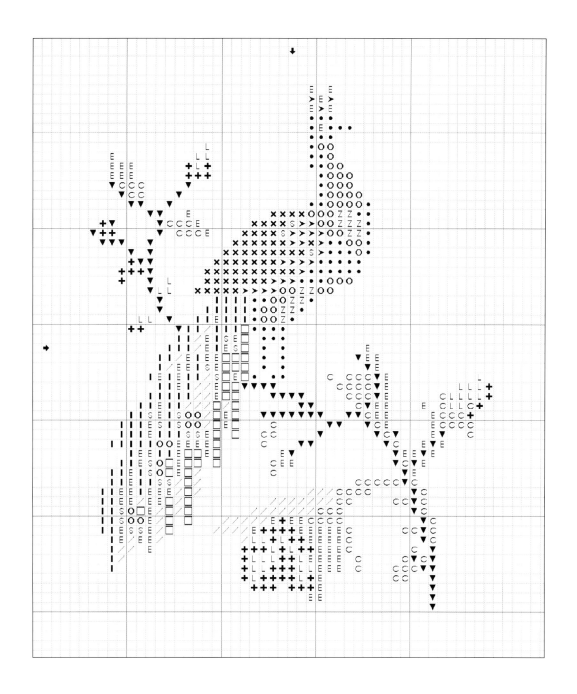

PROJECT #6.3
Bouquet of Roses
Designed by: Duffy Wineman

Materials Needed:
> #48 silk gauze
> DMC embroidery floss

Stitch Count:
> 51 (w) x 43 (h)

Color Chart:

Code	Color	Comparable to DMC #'s
✖	Vy. Dk. Shell Pink	221
➤	Dk. Shell Pink	3721
C	Med. Shell Pink	3722
╱	Lt. Shell Pink	223
V	Vy. Lt. Shell Pink	224
·	Ult. Lt. Shell Pink	225
●	Dk. Gold	680
─	Med. Gold	729
○	Lt. Gold	676
L	Vy. Lt. Gold	677
I	Off White	746
▽	Med. Blue	3755
U	Lt. Blue	775
✚	Dk. Green	3051
✕	Med. Green	3052
Z	Lt. Green	3053
☐	Black (Background)	310

Photo by Mary Kaliski

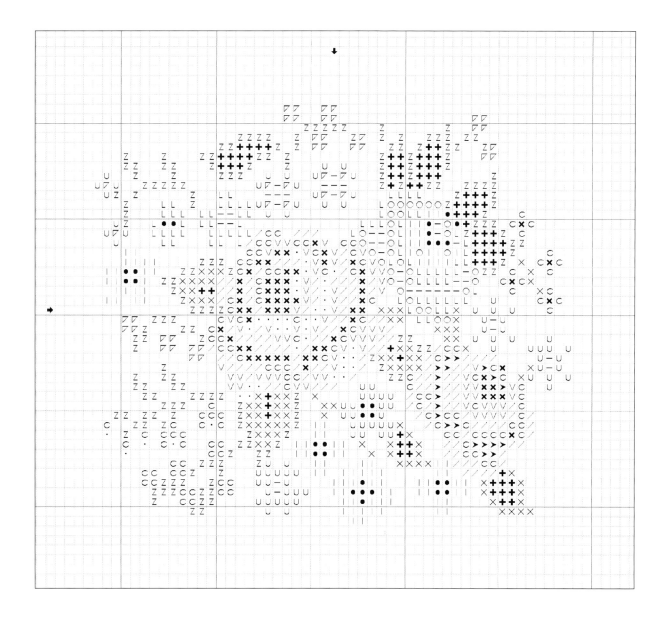

PROJECT #6.4
Victorian Bellpull
Designed by: Anne Chauvin

Materials Needed:
> #48 silk gauze
> DMC embroidery floss

Color Chart:

Code	Color	Comparable to DMC #'s
✖	Dk. Green	3362
S	Med. Green	3363
=	Khaki Green	3012
○	Dk. Rose	3721
I	Med. Rose	223
◑	Vy. Dk. Flesh	632
◓	Dk. Flesh	3772
▽	Med. Flesh	407
U	Lt. Flesh	3773
◣	Dk. Mauve	3802
T	Med. Mauve	726
B	Antique Mauve	316
+	Lt. Antique Mauve	778
−	Dk. Blue	3807
R	Med. Blue	793
✚	Dk. Gray Green	3051
▽	Terra Cotta	3830
●	Dk. Brown	3781
G	Dk. Olive Green	731
C	Fern Green	522
↗	Lt. Fern Green	524
△	Vy. Dk. Gold	3829
×	Dk. Gold	680
L	Med. Gold	729
8	Lt. Gold	677
▲	Vy. Dk. Topaz	780
➤	Dk. Topaz	781
Z	Med. Topaz	782
E	Lt. Topaz	783
▮	Dk. Violet	3740
K	Med. Violet	3041
#	Lt. Violet	3042
▼	Dk. Golden Olive	830
≈	Med. Golden Olive	831
≡	Golden Olive	832
□	Black (Background)	310

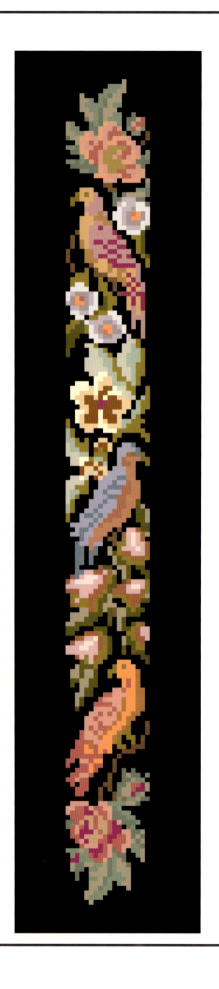

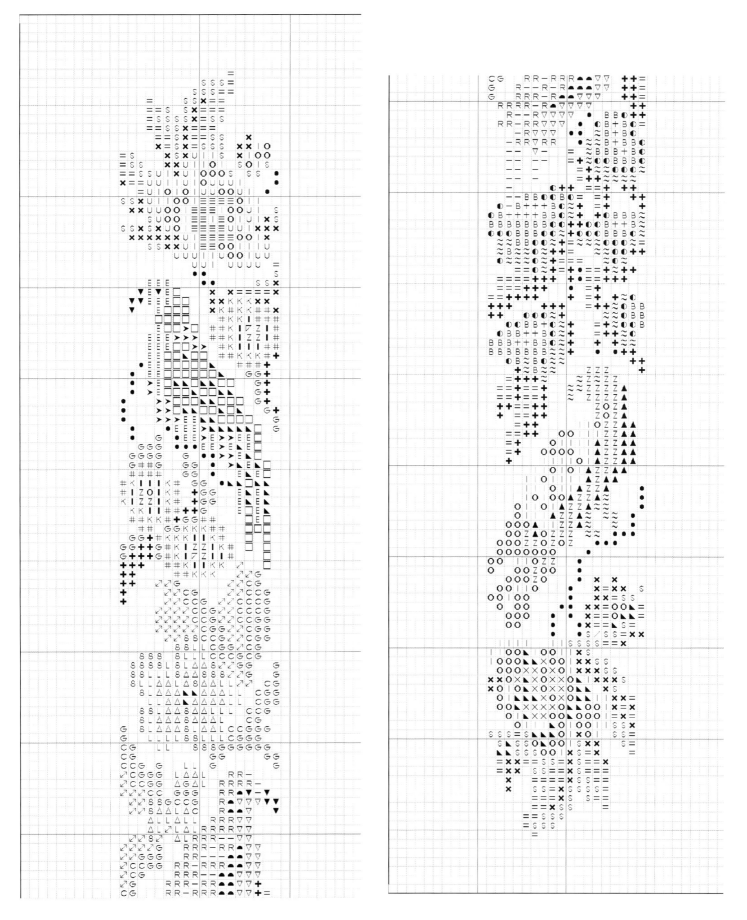

PROJECT #6.5
King Charles Spaniel
Designed by: Annelle Ferguson

Materials Needed:
> #48 (or smaller) silk gauze
> DMC embroidery floss

Photo by Mary Kaliski

Color Chart:

Code	Color	Comparable to DMC #'s
▼	Med. Brown	433
o	Lt. Brown	434
✕	Tan	436
●	Lt. Tan	738
C	Lt. Steel Grey	318
/	Pearl Grey	415
□	Ecru	
B	Dk. Terra Cotta	3830
S	Med. Terra Cotta	356
❙	Dk. Gold	680
–	Vy. Pale Gold	746
▼	Vy. Dk. Green	500
△	Dk. Green	501
□	Lt. Beige (Background)	842

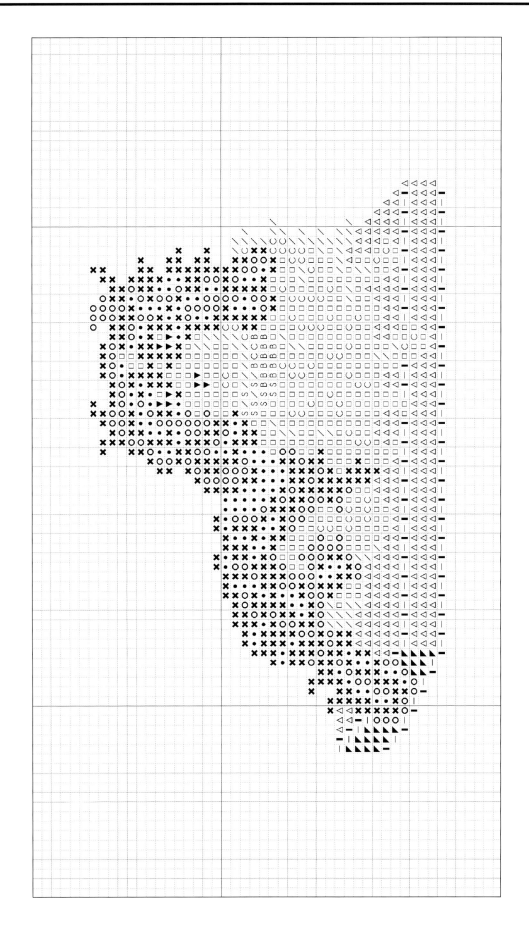

PROJECT #6.6
Slippers
Designed by: Bobbie Schoonmaker

Materials Needed:
> #60 silk gauze
> Silk sewing thread/embroidery floss

Code	Color	Comparable to DMC #'s
◢	Deep Rose	326
✘	Rose	899
○	Med. Pink	3326
●	Hunter Green	3347
╱	Med. Forest Green	471
☐	Black (Background)	310

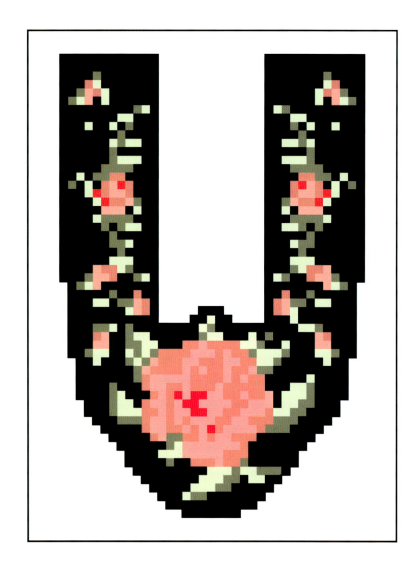

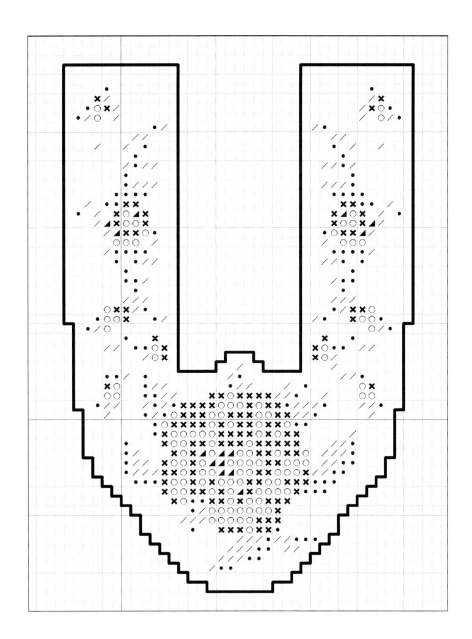

PROJECT #6.7
Victorian Floral Carpet
Designed by: Shirlee Greenberg

Materials Needed:
>   #40 silk gauze
>   Au ver à soie silk floss/
>   DMC embroidery floss

Stitch Count:
>   227 (w) x 315 (h)

Color Chart:

Code	Color	Comparable to DMC #'s	Au Ver A Soie
⦾	Dk. Mauve	315	4646
—	Med. Mauve	316	4634
Z	Lt. Mauve	778	4632
+	Vy. Dk. Garnet	902	4626
●	Dk. Garnet	814	4624
I	Terra Cotta	3778	643
▽	Lt. Terra Cotta	758	2632
E	Flesh	951	2911
▽	Dk. Salmon	947	2916
S	Salmon	3328	924
✖	Dk. Green	367	3425
╱	Grey Green	3052	3723
○	Lt. Grey Green	3053	3722
☐	Black (Background)	310	Noir

Photo by Mary Kaliski

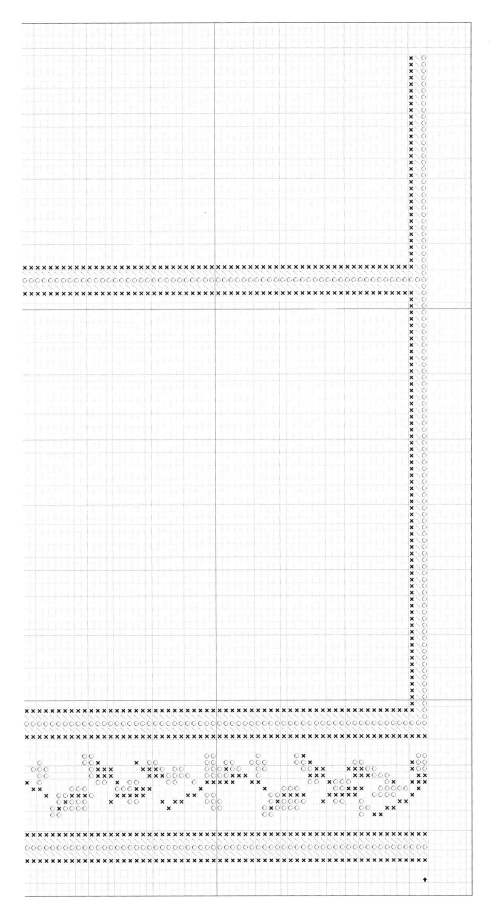

PROJECT #6.8
Lambrequin
Designed by: Judith Kaelin

Materials Needed:
> #35 Brussels linen
> DMC embroidery floss

Special Instructions:
Repeat side patterns until lambrequin
fits around side edges of mantel.

Photo by Mary Kaliski

Color Chart:

Code	Color	Comparable to DMC #'s
•	Lt. Tan	738
✖	Dk. Terra Cotta	355
○	Med. Gold	729
V	Med. Forest Green	989
◢	Dk. Forest Green	987
—	Peach	353
I	Dk. Violet	327
+	White	
☐	Black (Background)	310

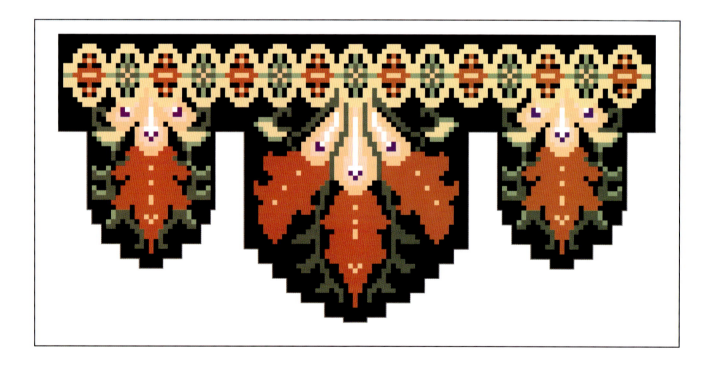

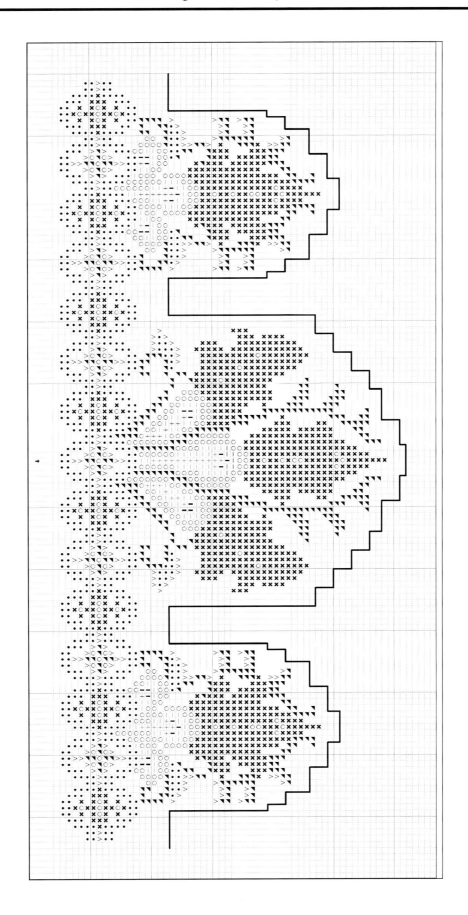

PROJECT #6.9
"Bristol-Board" Style Sampler
Designed by: Erma Scrimgeour

Materials Needed:

    #48 silk gauze
    DMC embroidery floss

Stitch Count:

    109 (w) x 49 (h)
    Finished size: 2½ in. x 1⅛ in.

Color Chart:

Code	Color	Comparable to DMC #'s
o	Dk. Green	937
✖	Dk. Brown	839
·	Med. Brown	611
●	Dk. Garnet	814
▽	Med. Garnet	815
=	Garnet	816
+	Red	304
Z	Vy. Deep Rose	326
/	Deep Rose	309
L	Rose	335
B	Med. Rose	899
C	Lt. Rose	3326
I	Med. Pink	776
□	Lt. Brown (Background)	613

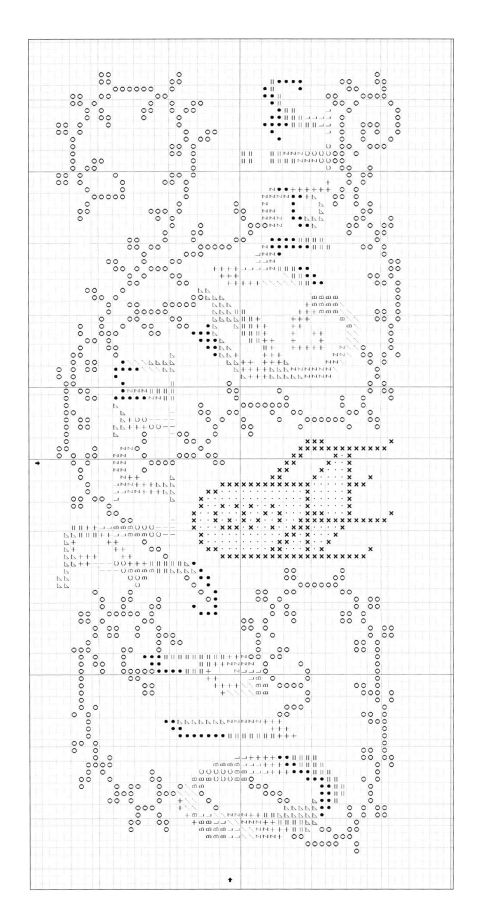

PROJECT #6.10
"William Morris" Wall Hanging
Designed by: Clarice Elder

Materials Needed:
   #28 black Jobelan
   DMC embroidery floss

Stitch Count:
   67 (w) x 103 (h)

Color Chart:

Code	Color	Comparable to DMC #'s
╱	Lt. Mustard	372
+	Dk. Hazel Nut Brown	420
×	Lt. Hazel Nut Brown	422
▽	Lt. Fern Green	524
○	Lt. Drab Brown	613
•	Vy. Dk. Flesh	632
∨	Lt. Beige Grey	822
▶	Dk. Yellow Beige	3045
−	Med. Yellow Beige	3046
➤	Dk. Flesh	3772

Backstitch using the following colors:
   Top center leaves: 420
   All other: 3046

PROJECT #6.11
William Morris Style Seat Cushion
Designed by: Anne Chauvin

Materials Needed:
    #48 silk gauze
    DMC embroidery floss

Stitch Count:
    73 (w) x 61 (h)

Color Chart:

Code	Color	Comparable to DMC #'s
✖	Dk. Mauve	315
•	Med. Mauve	3726
8	Flesh	3064
○	Dk. Brown	611
❙	Dk. Green	3051
∨	Khaki Green	3012
□	Beige	842

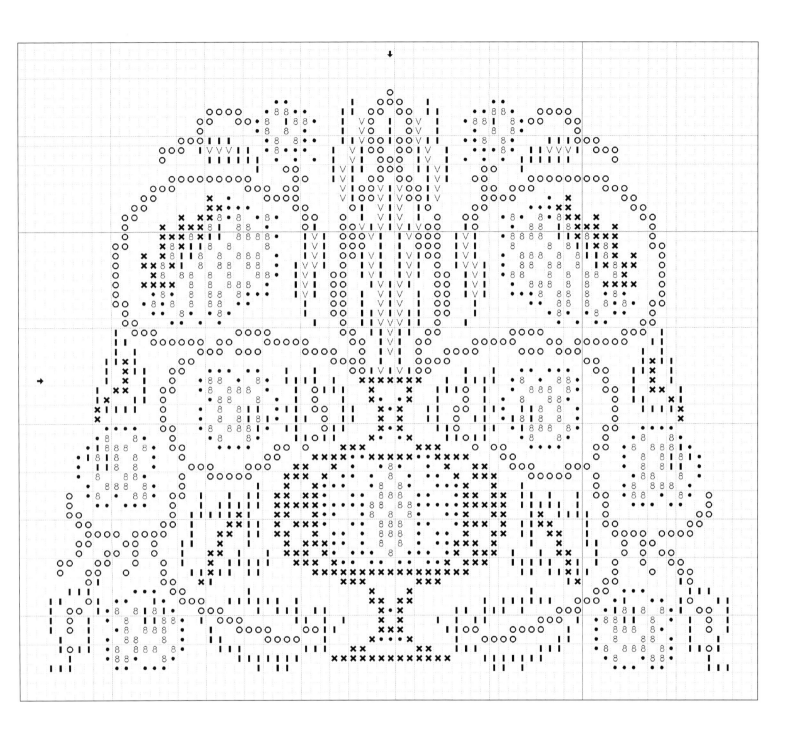

Gallery
of Needle Arts

Let each man exercise the art he knows.
—Aristophanes (450-385 B.C.)

Sue Bakker needlework is an interpretation of a popular 18th-century English design showing the "simple life" of an elegantly dressed shepherdess herding her sheep. Fire screen by David Booth. Neale Albert collection.

Needlework by Anne Chauvin in a Therese Bahl room setting. Chair seat on left in the style of a shell design stitched by Martha Washington and on view at Mount Vernon. Lolling chair by Roger Gutheil. DuRee Eaton collection.

Photo by Peter Charman

Ann Crompton's 1:12 scale needleworked picture worked on #112 silk gauze was Ann's winning entry to A World in Miniature needlepoint competition sponsored by David Kilpatrick of Oban, Scotland.

Susan Richardson wall pocket. Lynda Bauer collection.

Photo by Daemon

Rugs worked on #28 Jobelan by Clarice Elder.

Gallery
of Needle Arts

Photo by Daemon

Living room of Clarice Elder's dollhouse with Clarice peeking through the door. Rug design by Barbara Cosgrove, stitched by Clarice. Pillows designed and stitched by Clarice.

Collage of carpets, all worked on #40 to #60 silk gauze by Shirlee Greenberg. Shirlee does not chart her work; she simply needlepoints her designs.

Photo by Mary and Tom Kaliski

Gallery
of Needle Arts

Shirlee Greenberg needlework on #60 silk gauze. Donald Dube love seat with modified flame stitch. Rug is a replica of a full-size, prize-winning rug made by Shirlee. A Van Gogh painting inspired the needle-worked landscape picture. End table by Nicole Walton-Marble. Pottery by Andrea Fábrega.

Lucy Iducovich needlework, duplicate of an original French-style *pouf* (ottoman). Skirt fabric was taken from remnants of the original piece.

Judith Ohanian needle-worked the c. 1750 rual setting, *Wheatcutters*. Room by Pam Throop. Pat Arnell collection.

Gallery
of Needle Arts

Rosemary Hansen floral needle-work upholstery. Chair by Bob Chucka. Sarah Salisbury collection. (*Miniature Collector*, Jan./Feb. '97)

Berlin-style roses needleworked by Annelle Ferguson on Carol Hardy embroidery stand, Sandy Wall floral arrangement, Therese Bahl marbleized stand. Auction piece at 1996 IGMA show. Sarah Salisbury collection.

Photo by Jason Getzan

Photo by Mary and Tom Kaliski

Lucy Iducovich worked this Bakhtiari style carpet in #40 silk gauze. All squares have symbolic meaning.

Judith Kaelin's needlework: mullet-colored rug based on a fabric design, worked on 40 ct. Brussels linen; Indian dhurrie rug in blue and white, worked on 35 ct. Brussels linen.

Judith Ohanian needlework: *Baby Stuart* is an original design from a 17th-century portrait painted by Flemish artist Sir Anthony Van Dyck.

Photo courtesy of Esther Robertson

Esther Robertson's needleworked insert on #60 silk gauze is an adaptation of an Italian tapestry. Game table by Bill Robertson.

Photo courtesy of Esther Robertson

Esther Robertson's candle screen needlework is taken from the center motif of the game table at left. It is worked on #72 silk gauze. Candle stand by Bill Robertson.

Bobbie Schoonmaker needleworked a floral design in the style of Berlin wool work that was popular in 19th-century England and America. Embroidery/sewing stand by Maggie Urciuoli. Nell Corkin collection.

Photo by Mary and Tom Kaliski

Photo by Jason Getzan

Bobbie Schoonmaker needlework. The Chinese dragon design was a very popular pattern in 18th-century England. Footstool and embroidery hoops by Maggie Urciuoli of Small Ideas. Sarah Salisbury collection.

Gallery
of Needle Arts

Erma Scrimgeour needlepointed a map of Canada in blackwork.

Photo by Anne Day Smith

Photo by Anne Day Smith

Game table designed and constructed by Virginia Merrill. Inserted needlework panel designed by Susan Richardson. Seat covers by Virginia Merrill on chairs by Paul Runyon.

Photo by Mary and Tom Kaliski

Erma Scrimgeour's Bargello-style needlework on a chair seat. Murray Scrimgeour chair.

Pat Tulski's four contemporary design samplers are worked on #48 silk gauze.

Cookie Ziemba needlework: flame stitch on Betty Valentine slipper chair; needlework in progress on Betty Valentine embroidery stand; floral design on fire screen. Roger Gutheil end table.

Rugs in scales 1:12 to
1:144 by Sharon Garmize.

Living room with curtains crewelworked by Virginia Merrill. (*Miniature Collector*, Sept. '96, p. 26.)

English style floral needlepoint design by Annelle Ferguson on pole screen by Roger Gutheil. Peter Kendall collection.

Photo by Anne Day Smith

Jean Strup needleworked the bed coverings in the bedroom of Jackie Andrews's *Wilton* dollhouse. (*Miniature Collector*, Nov./ Dec. '95, p. 34.)

Photo by Mary and Tom Kalski

Griffin sitting on a cornucopia designed and worked by Mitzi Van Horn on #50 silk gauze. Frank and Lois Whittemore collection.

Mitzi Van Horn daybed cover and firescreen panel, Susan Sirkis doll in *Wilton* parlor. Jackie Andrews collection. (*Miniature Collector*, Nov./Dec. '95, p. 35.)

Gallery
of Needle Arts

IGMA clock case: William and Mary scene with Jean Strup's embroidered Stuart picture cabinet and Sharon Garmize's needlework-in-progress on a Judy Beals frame. (*Miniature Collector*, Spring '94, p. 22.)

Armchair and end table, Gerald Crawford; Bargello wing chair, Judith Ohanian; painting, Margaret Nine; silver bowl, Pete Acquisto; floorcloth, Ann Miller.

Gallery
of Needle Arts

Photo courtesy of Kansas City Toy and Miniature Museum

Photo by Emily Good

Therese Bahl painted room, Susan Richardson bench cover, Carol Hardy embroidery stand with Sharon Garmize needlework.

Emily Good hooked these rugs using a single strand of DMC floss and a punch needle. All are copies of antique rugs dated from middle to late 19th century.

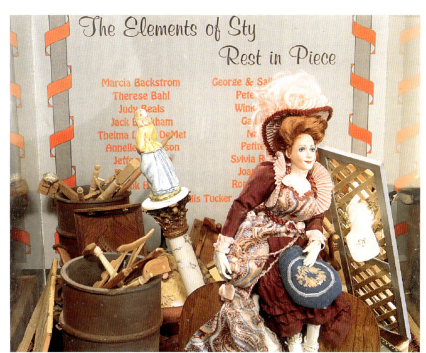

*Elements of Sty, (Miniature Collector, Jan./Feb. '97, p. 58.) Sarah Salisbury's collection. Scene created by Wink Knowles

Clock case with bargello seat cover stitched by Sarah Salisbury. Sarah Salisbury collection. (*Miniature Collector*, Jan./Feb. '97, p. 55.)

Gallery
of Needle Arts

Annelle Ferguson needlework within a George Hoffman roombox: needlework in progress on a Mark Caldwell embroidery stand; sampler interpreted and adapted from a 1690 English band sampler. Pierre Wallack bench, Anne Chauvin pillow, Cindy Malon rocker, Bearly Big Enough chest and table, Mary Hoot stuffed dog. Mary Kaliski collection.

Martha Crowe bargello on Roger Gutheil lolling chair, Sarah Anne Evans Oriental rug and faded sampler, Judith Ohanian pulled-thread sampler, Virginia Merrill embroidery stand.

Stitch Instructions

1. The coded stitches on needlepoint projects should be worked in the continental stitch. The uncoded stitches (background) may be worked in the basketweave stitch.
2. Using one (1) strand of floss, start designs at the center. Unless otherwise noted, all stitching is done with a single strand.
3. The needlepoint stitch is worked on the slant, covering one intersection of the threads of the canvas.

CROSS-STITCH
Cross-stitch consists of making a cross over each thread of the fabric.

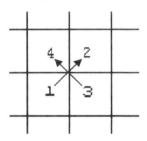

HALF/CROSS

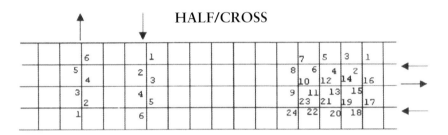

CONTINENTAL

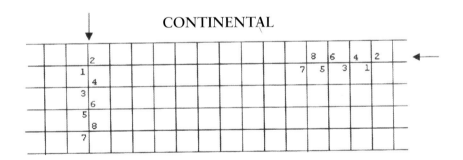

BASKET/WEAVE

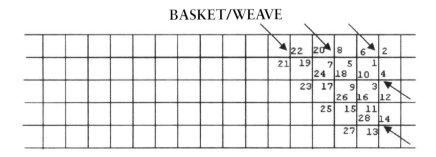

Special Note: On all needlepoint/cross-stitch patterns, each coded square on the chart represents one stitch on the fabric.

Bibliography

....God gives every man the virtue, temper, understanding, taste, that lifts him into life, and lets him fall just in the niche he was ordained to fill.
—William Cowper (1731-1800)

Bath, Virginia. *Needlework in America*. New York: The Viking Press, 1979.

Beard, Geoffrey. *The Magazine Antiques: Some Eighteenth Century English Seats and Covers Examined*. June, 1994, pages 842-849.

Benn, Elizabeth (Editor). *Treasures from the Embroiderers' Guild Collection*. United Kingdon: A David and Craft Book, 1995.

Bolton, Ethel Stanwood and Coe, Eva Johnson. *American Samplers*. New York: Dover Publications, Inc., 1973.

Cavallo, Adolph. *Needlework*. The Smithsonian Institution's National Museum of Design, Cooper-Hewitt Museum, 1979.

Clabburn, Pamela. *The Needleworker's Dictionary*. New York: William Morrow & Company, 1976.

Davis, Mildred J. *The Art of Crewel Embroidery*. New York: Crown Publishers, Inc., 1962.
_____ *Early American Embroidery Designs*. New York: Crown Publishers, Inc., 1969.

Digby, Winfield. *Elizabethan Embroidery*. New York: Thomas Yoseloff, 1964.

Edmonds, Mary Jaene. *Samplers & Samplermakers: An American Schoolgirl Art, 1700-1850*. New York: Rizzoli International Publications, Inc., 1991.

Fawdry, Marguerite and Brown, Deborah. *The Book of Samplers*. New York: St. Martin's Press, 1980.

Hanley, Hope. *Needlepoint in America*. New York: Charles Scribner's Sons, 1969.
_____*Needlework Styles for Period Furniture*. New York: Charles Scribner's Sons, 1978.

Harbeson, Georgiana Brown. *American Needlework*. New York: Coward-McCann, Inc., 1938.

Hedlund, Catherine A. *A Primer of New England Crewel Embroidery*. Massachusetts: Old Sturbridge Village, 1967.

King, Donald and Levey, Santina.*The Victoria & Albert Museum's Textile Collections: Embroidery in Britain from 1200 to 1750*. New York: Abbeville Press, Inc., 1993.

Krueger, Glee. *A Gallery of American Samplers*. New York: E. P. Dutton/Museum of American Folk Art, 1978.
_____*New England Samplers to 1840*. Massachusetts: Old Sturbridge Village, 1978.

Lane, Rose Wilder. *Women's Day Book of American Needlework*. New York: Simon and Schuster, 1963.

Parry, Linda (Editor). *A Practical Guide to Canvas Work from the Victoria and Albert Museum*. New Jersey: The Main Street Press, 1987.
_____*William Morris Textiles*. New Jersey: Crescent Books, 1994.

Rhodes, Mary. *The Batsford Book of Canvas Work*. London: B.T. Batsford, Ltd., 1983.

Ring, Betty. *Let Virtue Be A Guide to Thee: Needlework in the Education of Rhode Island Women, 1730-1830.* Providence: The Rhode Island Historical Society, 1983.
(Editor). *Needlework: An Historical Survey.* New Jersey: The Main Street Press, 1984.
American Needlework Treasurers. E.P. New York: Dutton/Museum of American Folk Art, 1987.
Girlhood Embroidery. New York: Alfred A. Knopf, 1993.

Schiffer, Margaret B. *Historical Needlework of Pennsylvania.* New York: Charles Scribner's Sons, 1968.

Sebba, Anne. *Samplers: Five Centuries of a Gentle Craft.* New York: Thames and Hudson, Inc., 1979.

Swain, Margaret. *Mary, Queen of Scots.* New York: Van Nostrand Reinhold Company, 1973.
_____*Embroidered Stuart Pictures.* United Kingdom: Shire Publications, Ltd. 1990.

Swan, Susan Burrows. *A Winterthur Guide to American Needlework.* New York: Crown Publishers, Inc., 1976.
_____*Plain and Fancy: American Women and Their Needlework, 1700-1850.* New York: Holt, Rinehart and Winston, 1977.

Synge, Lanto. *Antique Needlework.* United Kingdon: Blandford Press, 1982.
_____(Editor). *Book of Needlework and Embroidery.* United Kingdom: Wm. Collins Sons & Co., Ltd., 1986.

Weissman, Judith Reiter and Lavitt, Wendy. *Labors of Love.* New York: Alfred A. Knopf, Inc., 1987.

Wells, N.M. *The Life, Times and Work of the World's Great Artists: William Morris.* United Kingdom: Brockhampton Press, 1996.

Special thanks to HobbyWare, Inc., P.O. Box 501996, Indianapolis, Indiana 46250, for assistance with the Pattern Maker™ program used in this book.